CONQUERING
RHEUMATOID ARTHRITIS

An Illustrated Guide to
Understanding the Treatment
and Control of
Rheumatoid Arthritis

WILLIAM BENSEN, MD

WYNN BENSEN, BA

WITH SECOND OPINIONS FROM
MARTIN ATKINSON, MD
SIMON CARETTE, MD
J.D. ADACHI, MD
GUNNAR KRAAG, MD

1996
Empowering Press, Hamilton, Canada

Canadian Cataloguing in Publication Data

Bensen, William George, 1949–
    Conquering rheumatoid arthritis: an illustrated guide to understand-
ing the treatment and control of rheumatoid arthritis

Includes index.
ISBN 0-9697781-8-X

1. Rheumatoid arthritis — Treatment.   I. Bensen, Wynn.
II. Title.
RC933.B45 1996   616.7'22706   C96–931852–9

For distribution information contact the publisher:
Empowering Press
4 Hughson Street South, P.O. Box 620, L.C.D. 1
Hamilton, Ontario, Canada, L8N 3K7
Tel: 905-522-7017; Fax: 905-522-7839; e–mail : info@bcdecker.com

The authors and publisher have made every effort to ensure that the patient
care recommended herein, including choice of drugs and drug dosages, is in
accord with the accepted standards and practice at the time of publication.
However, since research and regulation constantly change clinical standards, the
reader is urged to check the product information sheet included in the package
of each drug, which includes recommended doses, warnings, and contraindica-
tions. This is particularly important with new or infrequently used drugs. Any
treatment regimen, particularly one involving medication, involves inherent risk
that must be weighed on a case by case basis against the benefits anticipated. The
reader is cautioned that the purpose of this book is to inform and enlighten; the
information contained herein is not intended as, and should not be employed
as, a substitute for individual diagnoses and treatment.

Printed in Canada

CONTENTS

ACKNOWLEDGEMENTS

We wish to thank our patients, health care staff, and colleagues from whom we continue to learn; the team at Empowering Press who challenged and encouraged us to put our experience into print; Dr. William Hazell who taught the wonderful common sense of biology; Dr. William Goldberg who has a genius for practical medicine; Beth Snowden, RN, for her help in developing chapter eight; and Steven Covey who made us aware that real change must come through new paradigms.

DEDICATION

This book is dedicated to my father, Dr. H.W. Bensen, (1915-1964), who before he died from rheumatoid arthritis, gave me a life of joy and hope; and to Wynn, Robb, Jay and Ryan who made it complete.

With the publication of *Conquering Rheumatoid Arthritis*, William and Wynn Bensen have just flipped on a light at the end of the tunnel.

The author's sensitive, yet unflinching, confrontation with one of the most dangerous of 100 types of arthritis will be an authoritative source of hope for the 300,000 Canadians with rheumatoid arthritis.

With Canada's healthcare paradigm in a state of flux, *Conquering Rheumatoid Arthritis* deftly defines the new lay of the land, provides a manageable road map, and delivers some sobering truths about a violent chronic disease whose socioeconomic cost is staggering.

This book is destined to become a rheumatoid arthritis bible. *Conquering Rheumatoid Arthritis* embodies a growing demand for unfettered information and strategies that clear the way for informed participation in day-to-day health care decisions.

If nothing could do it before, *Conquering Rheumatoid Arthritis* has skillfully put to rest the deep-rooted falsehood that arthritis inflammation and pain are inevitable burdens of old age that deserve to take a back seat to more acute, life-threatening diseases. According to the Bensens, "rheumatoid arthritis patients should be at the front of the line and never have to wait for treatment."

The authors don't beat around the bush, and their tone is anything but patronizing. They avoid using too much medical or technical jargon. They tell people what they need to know, at once confirming the severity of the disease, while at the same time offering assurances such as "you need not become crippled, lose your spouse, your family, your job, nor in fact need you die at a young age. In most people RA can be successfully treated, especially when treatment begins early ... It is the most significant treatable cause of disability in the Western world."

The authors also dare to explore some difficult facts about Canada's healthcare system with statements like this one: "Because of the way doctors are currently educated, arthritic diseases are poorly understood. A large proportion of medical training is directed to emergencies or to life-threatening diseases such as cancer or heart disease. Many doctors have little experience with how to diagnose and treat RA."

The "Common Questions" feature at the end of most chapters in the book reads like real-life visits to a doctor's office. The "Common Mistakes" feature keeps people on their toes too, with poignant statements such as this one: "Many patients feel that steroids are dangerous. This is a myth. Appropriately used, steroids make a real difference to how you feel and, potentially, to your arthritis."

Conquering Rheumatoid Arthritis is also chock full of straight shooting advice on medications and other therapies. Calculated, insightful discussions of drug side effects are also very useful. The book is particularly forceful in its identification of STAR$, the authors' certain-to-be-controversial ratings of nonsteroidal anti-inflammatory drugs. The Bensens also provide a bold, frank assessment of disease-modifying antirheumatic drugs.

Conquering Rheumatoid Arthritis is a welcome and valuable resource for people with RA and for those near to them.

Denis Morrice
President and CEO
The Arthritis Society

Rheumatoid arthritis (RA) is a tough disease. It can cause pain, swelling, and fatigue. It may profoundly affect your whole life—your job, your family, your leisure activities. It can even shorten your life.

Unlike cancer or heart disease, the media gives arthritis little attention. Within an ocean of diseases, arthritis is an iceberg—there is much more to it than is apparent on the surface. Rheumatoid arthritis can wear you down slowly, but treatment usually helps. Treatment is best at the beginning before the inflammation spreads, when the damage can be contained.

Unfortunately, RA has the reputation that it is incurable—that nothing can be done. Although RA is currently incurable, it certainly is treatable. However, most patients with RA get lost in a maze of options available for its treatment. While climbing the treatment pyramid, valuable time and the opportunity to control the disease without it causing irreparable damage is lost forever.

Health care systems are changing. The old system wherein physicians made all the decisions is gone. However, in the new system, patients, especially those with complex diseases, can be misunderstood. The choice and the responsibility, however, are yours! It is your health, and no one else will pay as much attention to it, or will benefit from it as much as you!

If you have rheumatoid arthritis, you need to be proactive. You have to initiate contact with your doctor and have the diagnosis made. You may need to get a specialist's opinion. You most certainly need to ensure that you receive appropriate treatment. Most of all, you need to become educated about your disease. The most important thing in the management of rheumatoid arthritis is to *get the disease under control.*

If the inflammation associated with RA is controlled, most of the other problems that occur as a result of the devastating effects of inflammation will never develop. Never accept that you have to live with it. Understand your treatment options and never accept treatments just because they are easily available. They may not work.

Fortunately, in Canada, patients have access to a national network with the Canadian Arthritis and Rheumatism Society, the Canadian Rheumatology Association (Physicians), as well as nurses and other allied health professionals who are dedicated to the management of rheumatoid arthritis. An active pharmaceutical industry offers patients and physicians education about the disease and is developing newer, more effective drugs. These drugs have a profound impact on the control of RA. When doctors work together with patients in clinical care settings and take advantage of research and education there can be a difference.

It is your life and your disease. Make the decision to get the treatment you need to get your disease under control.

William Bensen, MD
Wynn Bensen, BA

CHAPTER ONE

WHAT IS RHEUMATOID ARTHRITIS?

Rheumatoid arthritis (RA) is a really tough disease that can cause pain, swelling, and fatigue. It can affect your whole life—your family, your job, your leisure activities. It can even shorten your life. People dread RA and fear its reputation for causing disability or crippling. Fortunately, in most cases, RA can be controlled, and its effects on you and your future can be limited.

In this chapter we will talk about your joints, about arthritis in general, and about rheumatoid arthritis specifically. In the following chapters we will look at the different types of rheumatoid arthritis, at medical help, and at effective treatment for rheumatoid arthritis.

JOINTS

An important difference between you and a jelly fish is your skeleton: your bones and joints. Bones give your body its structure, and joints link your bones and allow your body to move. Without joints, your body would be like a statue. A joint is made up of the ends of two bones capped by a substance called cartilage and enclosed in a sleeve-like capsule. Most joint capsules have a lining called the synovial membrane, which has two main functions. Cells making up the synovial membrane release substances that lubricate the joint and they also remove debris resulting from regular wear and tear. Figure 1–1 shows the structure of a

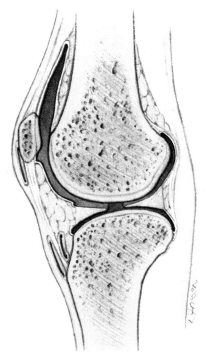

Figure 1–1: Structure of a normal synovial joint.

1

normal synovial joint. You can see how the bones are capped with cartilage and encased within a capsule lined by a synovial membrane.

ARTHRITIS

Arthritis means inflammation in the joint. Inflammation is painful and is a very common medical problem. Arthritis is not the same as arthralgia, aches or pains many of us feel upon awakening or after exercising. If aches and pains are like a light summer rain, arthritis is like a storm, and rheumatoid arthritis is like a hurricane.

Figure 1–1 shows the different joint tissues: bone, cartilage, and the synovial membrane. Different types of arthritis are caused by problems in different parts of the joint, just as your car can break down for many reasons. Damage to the bone leads to abnormal wear, destruction of cartilage, and inflammation. Damage to the cartilage leads to osteoarthritis. Rheumatoid arthritis results from inflammation of the synovial membrane, or joint lining.

There are more than 100 known types of arthritis. Some, such as RA, osteoarthritis, gout, pseudogout, and lupus are common, while others are rare. The prevalence of different types of arthritis varies by population, age, and gender. For example, osteoarthritis is more common in older people; RA and lupus are more common in women; gout is more common in men; ankylosing spondylitis is more common in some Indian tribes. Genetics, hormones, and age — all play a role in determining who develops arthritis.

Arthritic diseases have a real impact. They are the leading cause of visits to family physicians, Workers' Compensation Board claims, and long-term disability. Arthritic diseases are a major part of health care costs. It is impossible to measure the real cost of arthritis to patients, their families, and to society. Figure 1–2 shows how many Canadians are affected by arthritis.

Conquering arthritis would make a real difference in our society.

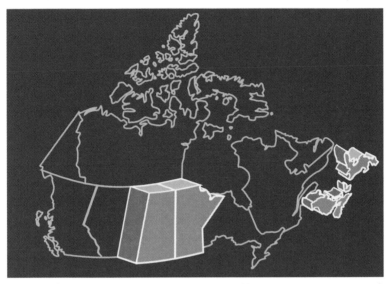

Figure 1–2 The number of adult Canadians affected by arthritis is equal to the combined populations of the highlighted provinces.

RHEUMATOID ARTHRITIS

Rheumatoid arthritis is one of the most common and serious types of arthritis. Rheumatoid arthritis affects all ages and all races. Overall it affects approximately 1% of the population, but it is two to three times more common in women than in men. The incidence of new cases is approximately 1 in 1000 to 1 in 2000 people per year.

Although RA can occur in children and teenagers, it normally begins between the ages of 25 and 60. However, RA can start in the 80s or 90s.

As RA appears to be more common now than in the past, it has been called a modern disease. However, RA is occasionally found in skeletal remains that are hundreds of years old. Rheumatoid arthritis apparently occurred more often in some ancient communities than in others. The idea that RA is caused by an infection has been asked.

Although the cause of rheumatoid arthritis is unknown, inflammation within the joint can permanently damage and even destroy the joint tissues. The damage and disability caused by RA depends on its type and on how quickly it is treated.

Many people believe that RA is incurable and that nothing can be done. In fact, the opposite is true. In most people RA can be successfully treated, especially when treatment begins early. However, because RA is still misunderstood, dangerous treatment delays may occur, and sometimes "quack" remedies are used.

Rheumatoid arthritis primarily affects the synovial joints of the body (Figure 1–3). Joints are usually affected symmetrically, or almost equally, on both sides of the body. Arthritis is often worse on the dominant side.

Rheumatoid arthritis is characterized by the

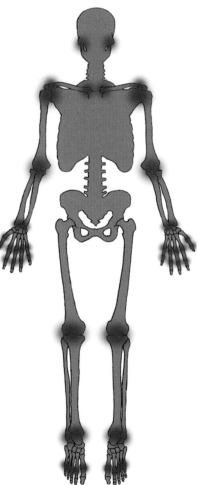

Figure 1–3: Synovial joints frequently involved in RA

signs of inflammation: pain, swelling, heat, and stiffness. Pain is caused by inflamed cells and chemicals that affect the nerve endings. In rheumatoid arthritis, pain is felt in the joint or with joint movement. Swelling is caused by thickening of the synovial membrane and sometimes by increased fluid or debris within the joint. Increased blood flow to the inflamed joint results in heat and redness. Stiffness, commonly called "morning stiffness," occurs in almost all inflamed joints after a period of rest or disuse. This is particularly common in RA. Morning stiffness can last from a few hours to all day long. To regain normal mobility inflamed joints must be loosened up by applying heat or doing exercises.

CAUSE OF RHEUMATOID ARTHRITIS

Although the specific cause of rheumatoid arthritis remains a mystery, there are clues which we will discuss below.

Infection or Diet

Although a great deal of research has looked at each of these factors, no specific infection, toxic chemical, or food has been identified as a direct cause of rheumatoid arthritis. Even though some patients may have a history of infection or chemical exposure the majority of patients do not. Almost all patients have done or experienced something in the weeks or months prior to the onset of RA that they feel may have caused the condition, but these factors appear to be incidental and unrelated.

Genetics

We inherit all our characteristics—physical, mental, and emotional—from our parents through our genes. Some genes make you more susceptible to developing certain diseases such as diabetes. Rheumatoid arthritis also has a genetic base, with most patients having an HLA-DR4 gene. This gene can be measured by a simple blood test. The HLA-DR4 gene is hereditary, making a family history of rheumatoid arthritis more common. Some forms, or alleles, of this gene may help predict the prognosis or outcome of rheumatoid arthritis.

Hormones

Rheumatoid arthritis affects women twice as frequently as men, probably due to hormonal differences. Interestingly, RA often recurs after pregnancy, or occasionally with hormone replacement. Although we do not understand the subtle interactions between hormones, the immune system, and the development of rheumatoid arthritis, we do know that a relationship exists.

Stress

Rheumatoid arthritis often develops after a period of stress. We do not know why this happens, but the joints can suddenly become swollen, painful, and stiff. We do know that stress affects the immune system and can significantly alter and even impair it.

Stress can be caused both by things that we can control and by things that we cannot control. All of us vary in our ability to handle stress. With a chronic disease such as RA, managing stress is even more important as it may help to control the arthritis. A simpler, less stressful life will often improve rheumatoid arthritis and decrease the need for drugs and medical therapies.

Environment

Certain environments make RA worse. Although the incidence of RA is similar in most areas, cold, wet climates with variable weather worsen the pain. Pollution may also have a subtle affect on RA. Many patients moving from a highly polluted city to the country may experience almost immediate improvement in their arthritis; decreased stress may also be a factor.

JOINT DAMAGE

Although we do not know the cause of rheumatoid arthritis, joint damage is caused by inflammation in the synovial membrane. This thin synovial membrane becomes inflamed and filled with cells called lymphocytes, macrophages, polymorphs, and fibroblasts. This thick, inflamed synovial membrane is called a pannus. The cells within the pannus become activated and release enzymes and chemicals that both permanently damage the cartilage and the bone and also attract more cells into the inflamed tissue. In rheumatoid arthritis, this inflammatory process is like a one way highway; the inflammation can continued indefinitely, causing more and more damage, possibly leading to joint destruction and deformity.

This inflammatory process is part of the body's immune system. The immune system is a natural defense against invaders such as bacteria, viruses, and even cancer. The cells of the immune system recognize and respond to invaders either by making antibodies to combat invaders or by attacking invaders directly.

Although the immune system is normally activated by a foreign agent, it can be activated to attack normal cells. In RA, for unknown reasons, the immune system becomes activated and causes marked inflammation in the synovial membrane. Many of the drugs used to fight RA have antibacterial and/or anti-immune system activity.

AGE AT ONSET

Rheumatoid arthritis may occur at any age, but RA most commonly begins during the 20s or early 30s, or later, in the 50s and early 60s. Both of these age groups are times of hormonal changes and high stress. The incidence curve for rheumatoid arthritis therefore looks like a "double-humped camel." The severity of rheumatoid arthritis also varies with age of onset. Onset after the age of 50 often means milder disease.

SUMMARY

Rheumatoid arthritis is a common disease with no known cause. It is the most significant treatable cause of disability in the Western world. If left untreated, RA may lead to severe damage and disability.

Fortunately, there is a window of opportunity for preventing disability in rheumatoid arthritis. If the disease is treated early, it can be controlled in most patients. Effective treatment depends on early recognition, a knowledgeable doctor, and proper treatment, which will be described later in this book. It is important for you to know that early treatment can make all the difference in the world, but treatment no matter when, will make a difference!

So you have developed rheumatoid arthritis (RA). Having RA means your life will change. However, you need not become crippled, lose your spouse, your family, your job, nor in fact need you die at a young age. What you do need is early and appropriate treatment, before the disease changes the course of your future.

Rheumatoid arthritis does not affect everyone in the same way. Just as different people have different personalities RA has different "temperaments". These "temperaments," or types, determine how RA can affect you personally and how it should be treated in your special case.

Historically RA was classified in terms of how it interfered with normal everyday functioning:

I.   Normal function
II.   Mildly limited function
III. Moderately limited function
IV.   Severely limited function (disabled),

and by bone damage caused by the disease that shows up on a x-ray film:

I.   Normal bone
II.   Some bone change
III. Moderate bone change
IV.   Extensive bone change.

This classification shows how much damage the inflammation associated with RA has already done, but it does not help to show how severe or how fast your RA will progress.

I suggest that the course of RA could be better classified by its "temperament" type:

1. Mild
2. Moderate
3. Severe,

and by its duration (how long it has been present):

1. Early (less than 2 years)—the best time for treatment
2. Progressive—the majority of patients at this stage have intermittent or steady progression of the disease and need continuing treatment
3. Controlled—when the symptoms of disease have subsided or have been successfully treated.

FACTORS AFFECTING RHEUMATOID ARTHRITIS

The character of the three main temperaments of RA are shown in Figure 2–1. When determining the type of your arthritis, we must consider the following:

1. *The severity:*
   Is the arthritis mild, moderate, or severe? Is it characterized more by "stiffening" than by swelling?
2. *The features other than those that affect the joints, or what we call extra-articular features (EAFs):*
   Extra-articular features are more often present in people with moderate or severe disease. They are usually absent in the mild type of arthritis. (We discuss EAFs later in this chapter.)
3. *The rheumatoid factor test:*
   The level of rheumatoid factor, an antibody found in the blood that has known effects in the immune system, is partially related to the severity of RA. Patients with moderate or severe disease usually have much higher levels of the rheumatoid factor than people with mild arthritis. Up to 20% of people with rheumatoid arthritis, however never develop a rheumatoid factor.

4. *The HLA genes:*

   The HLA genes are involved with the human immune system. The presence of different types of the HLA-DR4 gene may be important in predicting the type, the severity, and future course of your rheumatoid arthritis.

Figure 2–1: The three major temperaments of RA

Laboratory tests such as C-reactive protein (CRP), which measures inflammation, and the bone density test may also increase the accuracy of predicting the course of RA. However, as yet these tests are not used in everyday clinical practice.

In most patients, the type or temperament, of RA diagnosed at the onset persists during the entire course of their disease. However, in some patients, the type of arthritis does change. This usually happens early in the disease, before the full features of either moderate or severe RA have developed, making them difficult to distinguish from the mild form of the disease. Unfortunately, the disease most often "comes in like a lamb and goes out like a lion." The opposite is rarely true. It is uncommon for moderate or severe disease to become mild without treatment.

Mild Rheumatoid Arthritis

Thirty percent of patients have the mild type of RA. Mild RA is characterized by symmetrical joint inflammation (on both the right and left sides), pain, swelling, and stiffness, which usually occurs in the morning. Joint function is only slightly decreased. The only extra-articular feature is painful inflammation of the tendons (tendonitis).

In the mild type of the disease, the test for the rheumatoid factor is usually negative, or only slightly positive. No specific HLA genes are found.

In most patients diagnosed with mild RA, the arthritis remains mild throughout its course. In some patients, the disease may have only a very short course, but in others, it may recur intermittently or be constantly present for years. With the mild form of RA, damage or deformity of the joints is uncommon.

Moderate Rheumatoid Arthritis

Thirty to forty percent of RA patients have the moderate temperament of RA. Patients with moderate arthritis usually have much more pain, swelling, stiffness, and loss of everyday function than patients with mild disease. In moderate RA, the hands, wrists, elbows, knees, and feet are usually all involved. Often moderate RA is accompanied by early loss of movement and morning stiffness that can last from 1 to 3 hours. In cases of moderate RA, extra-articular features are common, particularly tendonitis. Many patients also develop nodules (firm, non-tender bumps under the skin, usually over the elbows, but also over other pressure points). Some patients may develop inflammation of their internal organs (which will be discussed later).

In cases of moderate RA, the rheumatoid factor usually, but not always, increases 2 to 5 times above normal. The presence of specific types of HLA genes may suggest unfavorable prospects for recovery.

If left untreated, moderate RA almost always leads to joint damage and deformity. However, patients with moderate RA have really benefited from disease-modifying antirheumatic drug (DMARD) therapy during the past 20 years, discussed in Chapter 4.

Severe Rheumatoid Arthritis

Approximately 10% of all RA patients are diagnosed with severe arthritis. Severe means *severe*. Severe RA is accompanied by marked swelling, marked pain, and marked joint stiffness. Normal function is profoundly affected. If you have the severe type of RA, you may not be able to hold a cup of coffee or move around the house. Deformity often occurs within the first few months. Sufferers of this type of RA feel tired, profoundly weak, and ill.

Severe RA is almost always accompanied by features other than those affecting the joints. Inflammation of the tendons is common, and most patients develop subcutaneous nodules. The internal organs become involved in the process of the disease. The rheumatoid factor is always strongly positive in severe RA. Blood tests usually show specific HLA genes are present, which suggests a very poor chance of recovery.

Without aggressive treatment, severe RA always leads to disability and possibly a shortened lifespan. In its early stages the severe form of RA can be confused with the moderate form of the disease. The distinction is important because patients with the severe form of RA must be aggressively treated if there is to be any chance of controlling the disease.

Rheumatoid Arthritis Associated with Stiffness

Ten to fifteen percent of all RA patients have the type of arthritis characterized by stiffness. This temperament of RA usually leads to abnormal tightness rather than to swelling in the small joints of the hands, wrists, shoulders, and occasionally, the knees and feet. The stiffness is marked. Although your joints may look normal, you may find it very difficult to hold a glass of water or to lift your arms above your head. Normal everyday activities can become impossible within a matter of weeks with this form of the disease.

With the exception of inflammation of the tendons (tendonitis), extra-articular features are rare in this type of RA. The rheumatoid factor test and the test for HLA genes are usually negative.

Loss of function is the major problem caused by this stiffness. You may find it very difficult to move and do things normally, and if left untreated this loss can be pronounced and irreversible.

JOINTS AND RHEUMATOID ARTHRITIS

As stated in Chapter 1, the major problem caused by RA is inflammation. The one-way progression of the inflammation may lead to permanent destruction if treatment is not started as soon as possible. In RA, inflammation affects different joints with different frequencies. In Figure 2–2, the joints *usually* involved are shown in red, those *often* involved in yellow, and those only *occasionally* involved in green. This pattern of joint involvement which is usually symmetrical (it affects both left and right joints), is typical of RA.

Tables 2–1 and 2–2 list the specific joint features that are most commonly affected by RA. Figure 2–3 shows RA of the left hand, and Figure 2–4 shows RA of the knee, and Figure 2–5 shows RA of the feet.

Extra-Articular Features of Rheumatoid Arthritis
The inflammation associated with RA also occurs outside the joints. These inflammatory changes are called extra-articular features (EAFs). Extra-articular features are more common in patients with moderate or severe types of RA

but they can occur in all types. Since RA can cause EAFs, it can be viewed as a disease that affects the whole body not just the joints. Extra-articular features can affect how you function, how you feel, and the quality of your life. A description of specific types of EAFs follows.

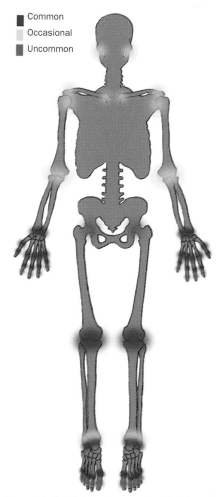

■ Common
□ Occasional
■ Uncommon

Tendons

The most common EAF in RA is tendonitis or tenosynovitis. Tenosynovitis is inflammation of the tendon sheath. Tendons, similar to joints, are often covered with a sheath-like membrane (the synovium). The synovium becomes inflamed and swollen in RA patients. Tenosynovitis occurs most frequently in the hands, but can also occur in wrists, elbows, shoulders, around the knees, and in the feet. Tenosynovitis is typical of RA

Figure 2–2: joint involvement with RA

and helps distinguish it from other types of arthritis, where extra-articular features are absent.

Nodules

In patients with moderate or severe types of RA, firm non-tender nodules develop under the skin, particularly in areas subject to pressure such as elbows, feet, or buttocks. These

Table 2–1: Arm Involvement in RA

	Hand	Wrist	Elbow	Shoulder
Frequency	Common	Common	Often	Occasional
Location	PIP, MCP	Wrist	Outside side	All over
Character	Pain, swelling, stiffness	Pain, swelling, stiffness	Pain, swelling stiffness	Pain—neck and arm
EAFs	Tendonitis (common)	Tendonitis (common)	Tendonitis (common)	Tendonitis (common)
Prognosis	Deformity, impairment of function	Deformity, impairment of function	Deformity, impairment of function	Impairment of function

PIP = Small middle joint of finger
MCP = Joint where hands join finger
EAFs = Extra-articular features

nodules are a hallmark of rheumatoid arthritis. They indicate that the more moderate or severe type of RA is present. In such cases, aggressive therapy is required. Nodules rarely occur with arthritic diseases other than RA. A typical under-the-skin (subcutaneous) nodule over the elbow is shown in Figure 2–6.

Table 2–2: Leg Involvement in RA

	Hip	Knee	Ankle	Feet (MTPs)
Frequency	Occasional	Common	Subtalar (Common) Ankle (occasional)	Common
Location	Groin Buttock	Front Back	Ankle, front sides	Under toes
Character	Pain Tightness Ache	Swelling Pain	Swelling Stiffness	Swelling Pain
EAFs	Bursitis	Baker's cyst	Tendonitis	Nodules
Prognosis	Stiff abnormal gait	Instability Weakness Baker's cyst	Fusion Stiffness	Deformity

MTPs = Joints where the toes joint the foot; Subtalar = Joints in the ankle that allow your ankle to move from side to side; EAFs = extra-articular features; Bursitis = Inflammation of a bursa, a synovial sack that lies between muscles; Baker's Cyst = Large bursa that lies behind the knee

Heart

The heart may become involved in RA. Inflammation occurs most commonly in the pericardium. The pericardium is a sac-like structure that surrounds the heart. The inflammation causes pain and occasionally an increase in fluid, which can compress your heart and impair its function. This type of inflammation (pericarditis) can be detected by a simple, ultrasound test. Only rarely does RA cause nodules or scarring within the heart walls, arteries, or on the valves of your heart.

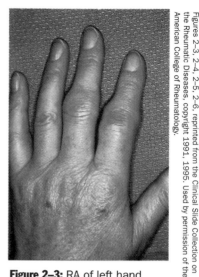

Figure 2–3: RA of left hand

Figures 2–3, 2–4, 2–5, 2–6, reprinted from the Clinical Slide Collection on the Rheumatic Diseases, copyright 1991, 1995. Used by permission of the American College of Rheumatology.

Lungs

With RA, inflammation of the lungs is common. The most common site of inflammation is in the pleurae, which lie between the lungs and the chest cavity. When the lungs are involved, most patients experience pain, particularly when breathing in or breathing out. In other patients, the pleural space, which separates the chest wall and lungs, fills with fluid. Occasionally RA patients develop nodules within the lung tissues, but usually these do not cause

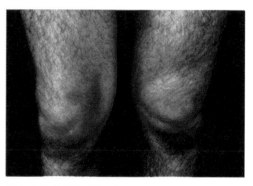

Figure 2–4: RA of the knee

Figure 2–5: RA of the feet

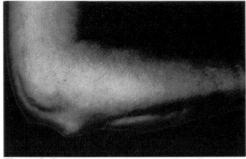
Figure 2–6: a typical nodule over the elbow

symptoms. Unfortunately, on an x-ray film, these tiny nodules may appear to be tiny lung tumors, and usually, a biopsy or other test must be done to rule out cancer. Occasionally inflammation occurs throughout the lungs. This condition of diffuse inflammation is called fibrosis and leads to lung scarring. Symptoms are shortness of breath and cough. Breathing tests help to confirm a diagnosis of fibrosis.

Nervous System

Rheumatoid arthritis can affect your nervous system. The most common cause arises from the compression of nerves. This occurs most frequently in the hands, and is called carpal tunnel syndrome. The carpal tunnel is a narrow shallow tunnel in your wrist through which all of the important nerves, tendons, and blood supply to the hand pass. Inflammation within this tunnel, caused by arthritis or other conditions, creates pressure on one of the nerves passing through it, which leads to irritation. Pressure on the nerve results in numbness in the palm of your hand and the second, third, and fourth fingers. Generally, the numbness in your hands is worse at night.

Rheumatoid arthritis can also affect nerves in other parts of the body. If RA causes damage to the joints in your neck, it can lead to bone shifts and compression of the spinal cord or the nerves that exit it. The result is numbness in the arms and legs.

Blood Vessels

In rare cases, RA can be so wide-spread that it causes inflammation within the linings of blood vessels. Blood vessel inflammation is called vasculitis. Damage to blood vessels or their closure can lead to damage in the organs that the blood vessels feed. Vasculitis is serious because it could damage organs such as your kidneys or your heart.

Eyes

Rheumatoid arthritis can affect your eyes, either directly by inflammation or, indirectly by damaging the tear ducts. If the tear ducts are damaged their secretions decrease, and you will experience dry eyes, particularly at night. Inflammation of the cornea can cause distorted vision and sometimes damage the eye.

CONSTITUTIONAL FEATURES OF RHEUMATOID ARTHRITIS

Many patients with the more severe type of RA feel ill, much as though they have a chronic bad flu. Patients feel tired, have no energy, feel nauseated, lose their appetite, and sometimes even lose weight. These symptoms are typical of RA and are called constitutional features. All patients with RA feel unwell, but patients with moderate or severe disease feel the most unwell. Like extra-articular features, the severity of these symptoms helps to separate RA from other forms of arthritis.

QUALITY OF LIFE AND RHEUMATOID ARTHRITIS

Rheumatoid arthritis will profoundly change your life. Most of us do not think about our health, until it is threatened. Hardly any one of us thinks about joint disease until pain, stiffness, and loss of function pointedly catches our attention. To live a normal life joints must function perfectly. Even minor joint disease causes dramatic changes. A joint disease, such as RA, which affects the whole system, may limit quality of life.

Quality of life is a medical term used as a measure of how you function and how you enjoy life. The term includes a sense of happiness and your sense of wellbeing. A sense of wellbeing involves your ability to interact with your partner and your family, to do your job, and to play with your children. Quality of life is an overall assessment with which each of us can easily identify.

Needless to say, if you have RA, the quality of your life is limited. A description of some of the ways in which rheumatoid arthritis can affect your life follows.

Joint Inflammation

We have already discussed in this chapter how RA causes marked joint inflammation. The resulting pain, swelling, stiffness, and loss of function will clearly add stress to your life. If you find moving, walking, or performing normal everyday activities difficult, your quality of life will be changed.

Extra-Articular Features

The extra-articular features of RA can also have an impact on the quality of your life. Tendonitis causes difficulty when you try to move your joints. If the internal organs become involved this can lead to a loss of function (e.g., if the lungs become involved in the inflammatory process, shortness of breath or loss of exercise tolerance can occur).

General Health

How the constitutional features of rheumatoid arthritis can make you feel have also been discussed. When you feel ill, nauseous, and tired, it is difficult to be cheerful, let alone accomplish what you want to accomplish. Interactions with your family and friends, even performing your job, can become difficult.

Drugs

In Chapter 4 we will discuss drug management strategies that help control RA. However, drug therapy is a two-edged sword. Whereas drugs have clear benefit in helping control the symptoms of arthritis, some can make you feel ill because of side effects.

Depression

Depression is common in patients with RA. Most of us are saddened by the difference between what we want to accomplish and what we actually do accomplish. This feeling is naturally much more pronounced in patients with RA. You may also be perplexed and wonder why RA has happened to you. Worse, if you think the disease cannot be controlled, you may feel a sense of hopelessness.

Early Death

Not only can RA affect your quality of life, it may even have the potential to shorten it. If you have the more severe type of disease with organ involvement, to resist or delay treatment may increase your chances of early death. Despite this severe outcome, rheumatoid arthritis does not receive the same attention as heart disease or cancer, which have gripped the public imagination. Diseases that kill slowly and diseases that kill quickly are perceived differently by the public. However, since RA may lead to an early death, the outcome is very important to you!

Employment

Rheumatoid arthritis may have a profound effect on your work. In these days of unstable and changing employment, this can be a problem. Joint inflammation, the constitutional features of RA, or depression may make some work impossible to do. Other work may have to be done more slowly. Interaction with your boss or with co-workers may be different, and your productivity may change. Having rheumatoid arthritis impairs your role in the workplace. It is one important reason why RA must be controlled as soon as possible.

Family

It is inevitable that RA will have a significant effect on your family. If a member of the family is suffering constant pain and is feeling unwell, it is only natural that relationships and normal family activities will be disrupted. Relationships with your spouse, your children, even with your extended family will change. Significant strain and stress may result, and anxiety about work or money matters may ensue. Previously enjoyable family activities may be curtailed or even become impossible. If this disruption of family life is to be minimized, RA must be diagnosed and treated as quickly as possible.

Sexuality

Sexuality is the glue that bonds relationships together. If you have RA, sex may become a problem because you are in pain, because you feel unwell, or because you are experiencing depression. People with RA may feel much like they have the flu, all the time, and most people without RA, but with the flu, experience a temporary loss of interest in sex. It cannot be emphasized enough how important it is for you to take control of your destiny before RA takes control of you.

SUMMARY

Rheumatoid arthritis is a tough disease. It hurts, it stiffens, it can wear people down. It can change the way you live your life, disrupt your family, and impact on your job performance and your leisure activities. It can even shorten your life. However, there is good news. In most patients, RA can be controlled, especially if diagnosed and treated early. To receive appropriate treatment it is important to: (1) Recognize and confirm a diagnosis of RA as soon as possible; (2) determine the type ("temperament") of your RA as soon as possible; and (3) initiate appropriate treatment as soon as possible.

Rheumatoid arthritis becomes a major problem, primarily when treatment is delayed.

As we have discussed, and as we will discuss again in the succeeding chapters, treatment of RA works best at the beginning before the "fire" of the inflammatory process has spread, and the damage done is irreparable. Your goal must be to make sure you get the proper treatment! Now!

COMMON MISTAKES

1. Not getting your disease type "characterized."
   If you and your doctor cannot determine what type of RA you have, you must get a referral.
2. Not getting the course of your disease clarified early (less than 2 years).
   Often, patients are classified as late, chronic, or active. These terms may mislead you into not seeking treatment. The term "progressive" is preferred! It implies treatment is necessary now! Treatment makes a difference!

COMMON QUESTIONS

Q: Does treatment really matter?
A: Treatment matters very much, especially in early and progressive cases. New drugs can halt the disease and the damage that it can do. Unfortunately, this message has not reached the public. Many people believe that nothing can be done for RA. Others believe that arthritis is destiny. With proper treatment, this is not

true! Remember that RA is a leading cause of disability, but it is treatable.

Q: Can I really die from RA?

A: Unfortunately yes, particularly if you have the severe type. Increased chance of death can equal the chance of death from heart disease and some forms of cancer. However, early drug treatment is much more effective and safer than in the past.

Q: Will I become crippled and disabled?

A: Probably not! With modern treatment, crippling and disablement is very uncommon. Your doctor should be able to help answer this question if he or she knows what type of RA you have.

CHAPTER THREE

CHOICES AND RESPONSIBILITIES IN
CONQUERING YOUR RHEUMATOID ARTHRITIS

T he major problem encountered in conquering rheumatoid arthritis (RA) stems from ineffective treatment applied too late. The solution to conquering RA comes with its early recognition and accessibility to a knowledgeable physician who can select and initiate appropriate treatment.

If you think you might have RA, see your doctor right away. This is the essential first step. You need to get your problem diagnosed and, if it is RA, to get treatment started. Currently, the medical system is overburdened, and not geared to quick diagnosis and early, effective treatment of arthritic diseases. As a consumer of the health care system and its services, and the person most interested in your care, you must take some of the responsibility for getting treatment started now. No one cares as much as you do about your disease, and no one will benefit as much as you will by having it successfully treated. Ultimately, the choice and responsibility in the management of your RA is yours.

If you *want* to control inflammation, prevent progression of the disease, and minimize long-term damage, you *must*: find a qualified physician whose character and competence you trust and have your RA correctly classified (characterized). Only then can you be started on an effective program of treatment.

The same approach applies not only to patients with early RA, but also to RA patients whose disease is progressive.

Health care systems are large, complex, and sometimes difficult for patients with chronic diseases to navigate. Some of the more important reasons why this is so, include the following:

1. Because of the way doctors are currently educated, arthritic diseases are poorly understood. A large proportion of medical training is directed to emergencies or to

life-threatening diseases, such as cancer or heart disease. Many doctors have little experience with how to diagnose and treat RA.

2. Time is the scarcest of health care commodities, and dealing with arthritic diseases can take a great deal of time—a difficulty in many current health care systems.

3. Doctors may be swamped with patients, and their waiting lists may be getting longer and longer. Patients with RA are competing for scarce health care resources. Insurance claims, government benefits, and Workers' Compensation issues all compete with RA for a physician's time.

Here are some suggestions to help you cope with the health care system and get the help you need to manage your RA.

1. **Call your doctor as soon as possible.** State your problem clearly to the doctor's staff member who answers your call (this person will probably be the one who prioritizes appointments). Women often explain their situation clearly, but men (many having little experience in dealing with health care workers) frequently understate the severity and significance of their problem. By "keeping a lid on things" and understating problems your appointment may be put off for months, not days, because a sense of urgency was missing in this important first call.

   When you are making your first appointment, find out whether the physician is comfortable and experienced in dealing with arthritis-related conditions. If he or she is not, ask for a referral to someone who is, so that you can get in touch with the right doctor the first time.

2. **Get an appointment quickly.** Doctors' waiting lists are getting longer and longer all the time. Although,

"Tuesday evening at 7:30" or "Friday morning at 8:00" may be the best times for you, if you insist on these slots it may mean that you will be fitted into a cancellation slot. It is important that you get this first appointment quickly. Insisting on waiting for a cancellation slot instead of taking the first available appointment may give the receptionist two messages: (1) Your problem is not terribly serious; and (2) it may be difficult to deal with you.

3. **Focus solely on your arthritis during your appointment.** You will not have been scheduled for an annual check–up. If you talk about other things that have happened since your last visit, your doctor may become confused about the real purpose of your visit, and the arthritis issue may become clouded. Talk about the arthritis!

4. **State the problem clearly.** Some patients overstate the degree of pain they are experiencing but most of us understate it. You may fear the doctor's response or hope that the doctor can sort out your problem with little information. Arthritis-related problems are difficult to sort out at best. If you are vague, you are less likely to be offered a solution. State the problem clearly. Give the doctor a chance to understand what is going on then he or she is in a better position to make a correct diagnosis, and begin treatment.

5. **Come to a decision.** After you have seen your doctor, a history has been taken, and a physical examination and tests have been done, discuss the investigation plan, possible therapy, and follow-up. Book the follow-up appointment before you leave the office.

6. **If necessary, ask for a referral to a specialist.**
Always remember that a referral is your right. When in
doubt ask for a second opinion.

Take on the responsibility of navigating through the
health care system. Remember the system deals best with
acute life-threatening illnesses; chronic illnesses often end up
at the bottom of a waiting list. Being at the bottom of such a
list with arthritis has dire consequences. Be responsible for
getting your illness diagnosed and treated. And remember,
RA patients have every right to be at the "front of the line"!

DOCTOR–PATIENT RELATIONSHIP AND PATIENT EXPECTATIONS

You have arrived at your doctor's office. Here is an outline of
what you should expect to happen.

History
The doctor will want to take a history about your arthritis.
What follows are some of the more important issues and
questions that will be raised:

Joint Inflammation.   The doctor will ask you the following: Which joints are affected? Is the arthritis symmetrical
(or equal) on both sides? Do you experience joint stiffness in
the morning? If so, how long does it last? Is there swelling?
How long have you had symptoms? How severe are they?
Have the symptoms changed in character or location? Have
you ever had anything like this before? Did anything occur
that seemed to trigger the symptoms?

Extra-Articular Features.   Are other features present
that would suggest RA, such as tendonitis, nodules, or symptoms suggesting involvement of the heart, lungs, stomach, or

skin? Are features present that would suggest a particular type of arthritis, such as psoriasis, or the skin rash associated with lupus, or nodules suggestive of gout?

Past Health.   The doctor will want to know if anything in your past health could relate to your current arthritic problem. Questions could include subjects such as prior surgery, any other significant illnesses you may have had, and drugs that you may be taking. Some drugs can cause an arthritis that looks much like RA. The doctor will ask for a list of all the medicines you are taking. If you have any allergies, your doctor will seek information about these also.

Family History.   Your family history is very important in RA. If one of your parents or siblings has the disease, you have a higher chance of developing it.

General Health.   Feeling generally unwell is characteristic of RA. If you have joint pain, but feel great, you could have something else. Your doctor will ask if you have lost weight recently, feel tired, noticed a decreased appetite, or feel generally sick.

Joint Examination

After taking your history, your doctor will usually take 5 to 10 minutes to examine your joints, something which is relatively easy to do. She or he will be looking for signs of inflammation within your joints. Inflammation can be detected by

- Tenderness with pressure over a joint,
- Swelling,
- Pain (when you move the joint through a full range of movement, pain is experienced towards the end of the range),
- Redness.

The number and severity of inflamed joints, whether or not the inflammation is symmetrical, gives the doctor a sense of what type of arthritis you may have. The presence or absence of features such as tendonitis or nodules is also important and helps the doctor decide on the type of arthritis you have and its severity. If damage or deformity has occurred, these help in predicting the type and course of the disease (progressive or controlled) as well.

Remember, rheumatoid arthritis is only one of over 100 arthritic diseases. Many other diseases can mimic RA. These other diseases include osteoarthritis, gout, lupus, psoriatic arthritis, viral arthritis, haemochromatosis, pseudogout, and even fibromyalgia. Your doctor will be aware of these other forms of arthritis and, with the history and physical examination, will come to some conclusion about whether or not you have RA.

Laboratory Tests

Blood tests are helpful in diagnosing RA, but your history and physical examination are much more important. A description of some of the blood tests that are useful in diagnosing RA follows:

1. Erythrocyte Sedimentation Rate

   The most accurate and most often used measurement of inflammation is the erythrocyte sedimentation rate (ESR) (often referred to as the "sed rate"). This test is based on how quickly red blood cells settle out on the bottom of a test tube. In inflammatory conditions of any type (arthritis included), red blood cells settle out more quickly. The ESR is useful in differentiating RA from other types of arthritis.

2. Rheumatoid Factor

   Eighty percent of patients with RA have an increased

level of the rheumatoid factor in their blood. The rheumatoid factor is an antibody that is elevated in most patients with RA. An elevated rheumatoid factor is consistent with, but does not prove, that RA is present. However, a negative rheumatoid factor, particularly early on in the disease, does not exclude RA.

Most patients with moderate or severe RA develop a positive rheumatoid factor within the first 6 months to 1 year of contracting the disease. Some patients with a family history of RA will test positive for the rheumatoid factor all of their lives. The more positive the test, the greater the likelihood of RA being present. However, most doctors have seen patients with strongly positive tests and no other evidence of arthritis. Unfortunately, early on in the disease, and in patients with the mild form of the disease, the rheumatoid factor is often very low, or even negative.

3. Antinuclear Antibody Testing

An antinuclear antibody test is often used to screen for rheumatoid arthritis and other connective tissue diseases such as lupus. Antinuclear antibodies are antibodies that attach to the nuclear material of cells. A positive result may help diagnose if an inflammatory disease is present or not. However, the antinuclear antibody test is often positive, without any underlying disease.

4. Synovial Fluid Assessment

If your joints are very swollen, your doctor may take a small amount of fluid from the swollen joint for examination. Normal synovial fluid is clear, thick, and oily, which helps it lubricate the joints. In RA, the fluid becomes cloudy because it is infiltrated with cells, usually white blood cells, and debris. These cells break down the oily substance (hyaluronic acid) and make it very watery. By looking at the fluid, the physician can tell if it is normal or if inflammation is present. In a laboratory, the presence of inflammation can be determined.

DIAGNOSIS

After the first visit, your doctor will make a diagnosis based on your history, your joint examination, and your lab test results. In most patients, RA is easily identified. However, in some patients the diagnosis may be more difficult and delayed.

After making a diagnosis, the doctor will decide which type ("temperament") of RA you have and determine its course. Active or progressive arthritis must always be treated to stop the progression. To treat early (in fewer than 12–18 months) is always preferable, but treatment of all progressive RA, at anytime, is important. When doctors use the term "late" or "already damaged," the implication is *not* that nothing can be done. Nothing could be further from the truth. Rheumatoid arthritis should always be treated, and the earlier, the better.

TREATMENT

After making a diagnosis, your doctor will prescribe some form of treatment, usually a combination of drugs and supportive therapy. The treatment will take a few weeks before the effects are felt, at which point a follow-up appointment should be scheduled. Ensure that you understand the treatment plan before you embark on it.

If your doctor thinks that in your case, RA is even a possibility, set up a regular follow-up schedule so that the disease and its treatment can be closely monitored. Currently, most patients are seen only occasionally, over a period of weeks and months, while trying different drugs. If, after an appropriate period of time (up until 1 year), the disease is not brought under control, the patient is usually referred to a specialist. This is usually too late for a good outcome.

The major problem in RA is delay! Delays caused by lack of a diagnosis, long waiting lists, and inappropriate treatment, which mean that the "window of opportunity" to control moderate or severe disease is missed. Your persistence is needed to ensure that you get prompt and appropriate medical care.

MANAGEMENT

Figure 3–1 shows the five levels of RA management: level one represents the onset of RA; level two, the family physician; level three, the rheumatologist; level four, the institution of disease-modifying antirheumatic therapy; and level five, control. The left side of the pyramid indicates the many steps to be climbed between the onset of the disease and its control. Many patients become lost or take too much time negotiating these steps. On the right side of the pyramid a more useful paradigm shows patients on escalators. Their disease has been recognized early and treated with minimal delay. This chapter is really all about how to get on the escalator rather than the stairs.

The point made over and over is that it is you who must take on the responsibility of managing your RA. Moving quickly from disease onset to disease control is so important.

Rheumatoid arthritis is a serious and usually controllable disease. The solution to its effective management begins with early recognition and access to a knowledgeable doctor. Once RA has been recognized, your physician can apply the treatment principles and treatment modalities most suitable for your particular type and course of disease. We will be discussing these in the next chapter.

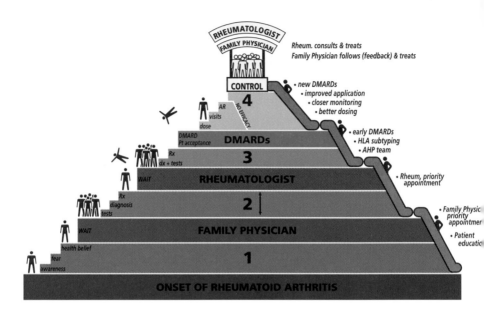

Figure 3–1: The RA management pyramid

The choice to get treatment is truly yours. Many patients, at the onset of their disease, fear that nothing can be done or distrust the medical system as a means to help them get the right things done. Even if you do not trust the system, getting an opinion is important! All information is useful and with time, may help you to make appropriate decisions.

Clearly, early recognition and diagnosis of RA is important to its successful management. It is also essential to deal with a knowledgeable doctor with a specific expertise and interest in arthritis. Once dealing with your case, this doctor will apply the principles we will review in the next few chapters. These will address how to control your disease and prevent it from progressing.

SUMMARY

This chapter continued to show the serious, but treatable, nature of RA. You as the patient will have the greatest interest in getting the most effective treatment for your RA. To accomplish this goal, your arthritis must be diagnosed promptly and its type determined. You need a knowledgable and interested doctor who is able to select and recommend the most appropriate treatment.

Take responsibility for your disease and navigate through the health care system to ensure your disease gets the treatment it needs. Rheumatoid arthritis patients should be at the "front of the line" and never have to wait for treatment. As Winston Churchill once said, "never give in, never, never..."

COMMON MISTAKES

1. Not knowing that recognition and early diagnosis of your RA is important.

    Delayed diagnosis results in delayed treatment, and delayed treatment results in more damage and deformity.
2. Not getting seen early enough by your doctor or rheumatologist!

    A common perception among the public is that, in medicine, a "first come—first serve" policy is in place. Make sure your case gets "to the front of the line." You are the patient; you take the responsibility.
3. Being too vague with your complaints.

    When you do get that important first appointment, do not expect your doctor to figure it out without your help. You are the one experiencing the symptoms. Be direct! Tell it like it is!
4. Delaying treatment.

    Do not assume that your symptoms will go away on their own! It is usually better to start treatment as soon as possible. If your symptoms disappear, you can always discontinue treatment later.

COMMON QUESTIONS

Q: My doctor says I have RA, but should I wait and see before trying any drugs?

A: Ask for a referral to a rheumatologist. Delaying treatment is usually wrong.

Q: My doctor says RA cannot be cured. Is this true?

A: Your doctor is right. It cannot be cured, but it almost always can be controlled. Can diabetes be cured? No, but treating it makes a real difference. Can high blood pressure be cured? Usually not, but controlling it can save your life.

Q: What should I do if my doctor is not sure if what I have is RA?

A: Ask for a referral to a specialist. Knowledge is power. You need to know now! Sometimes you cannot be sure you have RA, but you must have a knowledgeable doctor tell you this.

A SECOND OPINION

Rheumatoid arthritis affects about 1% of the adult population worldwide. This chronic disease strikes people of every age, sex, and ethnic group although some are at greater risk than others. Being Female is also a risk factor since rheumatoid arthritis disease affects approximately three times as many women as men. The disease may strike in any decade, but the onset is most frequent among those between 40 and 60.

The cause of rheumatoid arthritis is unknown. It is possible that many different infectious agents may activate the immune response in a genetically susceptible host. Currently, no strong evidence exists to single out any single infectious agent, or agents, as a key factor in the cause of rheumatoid arthritis.

For many years, since it is not directly lethal, rheumatoid arthritis was considered a relatively benign condition. With increased knowledge of rheumatic diseases, however, this assessment has changed. We now know that rheumatoid arthritis is a severe progressive disease that exacts a huge toll on patients, on the economy, and on the health care system.

Rheumatoid arthritis is a medical emergency. It is now generally accepted that the first 2 years of persistent joint inflammation is the time when most joint damage occurs. Thus, a narrow "window of opportunity" exists to alter the prognosis for most patients in this crucial, early destructive phase when the disease is at its most aggressive stage.

It was traditionally taught that 70-80% of patients with rheumatoid arthritis could be "controlled" with a first-line nonsteroidal anti-inflammatory drug (NSAID). These NSAIDs were given on the premise that most people with rheumatoid arthritis would, with time, go into a spontaneous remission. Second-line drugs such as Gold, Penicillamine, Methotrexate, or antimalarials were considered "highly toxic" and were reserved for those patients who could not be controlled with first-line therapies. We now know that spontaneous remissions are not common, and this traditional conservative approach to the patient with rheumatoid arthritis misses the "window of opportunity" to alter prognosis for most patients in this crucial early destructive phase, when the disease is most aggressive.

Today, rheumatologists recognize the urgency of treating rheumatoid arthritis early and aggressively. Only if patients are seen early in the course of the disease, and if effective treatment is instituted, will there be a chance to affect the prognosis of this disease.

Martin H. Atkinson, M.D. F.R.C.P.C.
Professor of Medicine,
University of Calgary.

CHAPTER FOUR

CAN YOUR RHEUMATOID ARTHRITIS BE CURED?

Currently, rheumatoid arthritis (RA) cannot be cured. However, in almost all patients, the disease can be significantly controlled. The major underlying feature of RA is inflammation. By controlling the inflammation, not only can the symptoms or RA be alleviated, but permanent disability (even crippling) can be prevented or minimized.

Three types of drugs help combat inflammation. One type of drug is sometimes prescribed alone, but usually several different types of drugs are used in combination. The help of local support groups and allied health care professionals is also of great benefit. The major aim of treating RA is simple: To control the inflammation—to put out the "fire."

If the "fire," the inflammation, of RA is put out, pain and swelling disappear, and damage and deformity are limited. Free of inflammation, you will be able to resume a more satisfying family life and return to work.

DRUG TREATMENT IN RHEUMATOID ARTHRITIS

The three major drug groups used in the management of rheumatoid arthritis will now be introduced. Each group will be discussed further in the chapters that follow.

Nonsteroidal Anti-Inflammatory Drugs

Nonsteroidal anti-inflammatory drugs (NSAIDs) (pronounced N-sayds) suppress inflammation and control pain. More than 20 NSAIDs are currently available. In my opinion only seven of these are what I will refer to as STAR$. Analgesic drugs such as acetaminophen may be added to prescribed NSAIDs to provide more pain relief.

Disease-Modifying Antirheumatic Drugs

Sometimes called "second-line" drugs, disease-modifying antirheumatic drugs (DMARDs) (pronounced Dee-mards) control the progression of the inflammation involved in RA in a unique way. The reasons for their action are unknown, but reputable drug trials have demonstrated that DMARDs suppress the disease and limit joint damage. Disease-modifying antirheumatic drugs are usually taken together with NSAIDs. Two DMARDs may be prescribed in combination. It is critical that DMARDs be used early in treatment of RA, because DMARDs are the most important drugs to take.

Steroids

Steroids produce potent anti-inflammatory effects. When combined with NSAIDs and DMARDs, steroids can control both the disease process and the inflammation. The remarkable ability of steroids to control inflammation makes them especially important for the early treatment of RA because NSAIDs and DMARDs need time to build up potency in your system. Recently steroids have been proven to prevent progression in RA as well as to relieve inflammation.

Over the past 20 years, new, safer drugs have profoundly changed the management and course of RA. Two decades ago, the majority of RA patients were unable to get their disease under control. Now, new drugs, used early, and in combination, control almost all RA in almost all patients. In most cases, the progression of the disease is stopped or slowed. The radical change in outcome, from disease progression to disease control, is wonderful news for RA patients. Suffering with little hope has been changed to joy through regained health and strength.

TREATMENT PLAN IN RHEUMATOID ARTHRITIS

Figure 4–1 illustrates the "treatment target" as a plan for treating RA. The diagram looks something like an archery target; its rings represent the drug groups: NSAIDs, DMARDs, combinations of DMARDs, and experimental and older drugs. Bands across the target represent supporting allied health care professionals and steroids.

If you look at the target, you will see that the different colours in each of the rings represent the different groups of drugs.

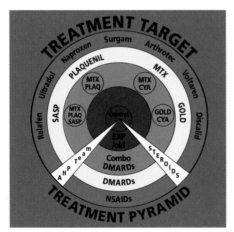

Figure 4–1: The treatment target

1. The green ring represents nonsteroidal anti-inflammatory drugs (NSAIDs). Over twenty NSAIDs are currently available but, as we will discuss further, seven of these are what I refer to as the STAR$.

2. The gold ring represents the disease-modifying antirheumatic drugs (DMARDs). These drugs are able to suppress the disease process. The four that I consider most useful are used first, and are shown in this ring.

3. The orange ring represents DMARDs used in combination. Combinations of DMARDs may work better and longer when used with other drugs. The benefits of combinations are becoming increasingly important in people with severe or aggressive disease.

4. The red ring represents experimental and older DMARDs. This ring represents the new, still experimental DMARDs, which are being developed and tested. These drugs may be conventional DMARDs being used in different ways or some of the new biological agents used to selectively treat some of the mediators of inflammation. Although these drugs are experimental, they offer hope for patients for whom treatments from the first three rings have failed. Some of the older DMARDs are still available; however, their power to control RA is not equal to the DMARDs represented in the gold ring. These drugs may be more toxic, or less efficacious, or more expensive but simply have not gained general acceptability. These drugs can be used when the best DMARDs fail.

SUMMARY

The main goal of treating RA is to control inflammation—to put out its "fire." The treatment target shows the three types of drugs used to manage RA (the different alternatives are shown within each treatment ring). At the bottom of the target, between the supports of allied health care professionals and steroids, we will develop selective treatment pyramids to fit each type of RA.

Nonsteroidal anti-inflammatory drugs, DMARDs, and steroids, usually in combination, are the three drug groups used in the treatment of RA. For greater effectiveness, your doctor may prescribe these drugs in concert much in the same way as a conductor leads an orchestra. Working together with your doctor, you will discover the proper proportions and achieve harmonious balance among these drugs to conquer your RA.

COMMON MISTAKE

1. Thinking that the management of RA is too complicated.
   You have a choice of three drug groups (some options within each), your doctor, allied health professionals, and self-help groups. These resources will help you sort out the best treatment to control your RA. Never quit!

COMMON QUESTION

Q: I have read about the pyramid approach to RA, why do I not see it here?

A: You will. The traditional pyramid approach to the treatment of RA is now considered too simple given our current understanding of various drug therapies. Different types of RA need different "pyramids." The new approach is further explained in Chapter 9.

CHAPTER FIVE

NSAIDs: THE FIRST LEVEL RHEUMATOID ARTHRITIS TREATMENT

Nonsteroidal anti-inflammatory drugs (NSAIDs) are the first level of therapy for most arthritic diseases. All NSAIDs lower fever, relieve pain, and reduce inflammation. Currently, 20 NSAIDs of different chemical groups are available; there are more than 50 ways of prescribing them: orally, as creams, or suppositories, and many different dosages are used.

The dramatic increase in the number of NSAIDs during the past 20 years has been a double-edged sword. Although the newer drugs have clear benefits when compared to the drugs ASA, phenylbutazone, and Indocid (indomethacin), available 2 decades ago, yet the large number of NSAIDs, the many dosing choices, and the lack of comparisons between NSAIDs have confused both patients and their doctors. The common perception that these drugs are equally effective in treating rheumatoid arthritis is *wrong*. In my opinion, some of these drugs are clearly superior or NSAID "STAR$".

Figure 5–1 shows the life cycle of a typical NSAID. Initially, the NSAID is introduced and marketed as the "new cure for arthritis." The drug then goes through a cycle of

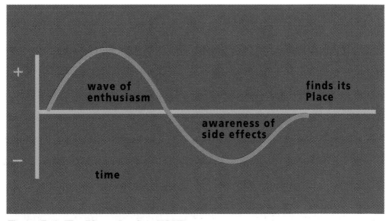

Figure 5–1: The life cycle of an NSAID

increasing acceptance and wide use, particularly by people who have tried every other drug available. Over time, the drug's side effects become commonly known, and the drug ceases to be perceived as a "cure." Typically, over a 1- to 3-year period, the drug finds its true place.

Although the exact way in which NSAIDs control inflammation is unknown, NSAIDs appear to affect several processes:

1. Prostaglandin production.

    Prostaglandins are the "currency" between cells in the body. Prostaglandins are often increased in inflammatory diseases, such as rheumatoid arthritis. Nonsteroidal anti-inflammatory drugs stop or slow the enzymes that make prostaglandins, thus helping to control inflammation. Unfortunately, other organs, such as the stomach, depend on prostaglandins for healing. Newer NSAIDs selectively slow "inflammatory prostaglandins" more than those in the stomach.

2. Cellular processes and interactions.

    Nonsteroidal anti-inflammatory drugs appear to modify cellular processes, making cells act and interact differently, leading to less inflammation.

3. The brain.

    Nonsteroidal anti-inflammatory drugs have direct effects on the brain to control inflammation.

Although NSAIDs have many actions, most importantly, they decrease inflammation and relieve pain.

IMPORTANT FEATURES OF NSAIDs:

Nonsteroidal anti-inflammatory drugs are all different; they have different chemical formulas. Therefore, their actions in different patients depend on the disease and the dose. They are also different in terms of effectiveness, side effects, and ease of use. These factors are important considerations when choosing of a NSAID. Some NSAIDs are "STAR$." They will out perform the rest because they have better profiles. We can create a profile for each NSAID by looking at the following important factors: Simplicity, Tolerability, Adverse Reactions, Relative Effectiveness, and $ Cost (STAR$).

NSAID STAR$

S = Simplicity
Some NSAIDs have simpler dosing schedules than others. It is much easier to remember to take one or two pills a day than to take three pills every 4 hours. No one seems to remember to take pills more than twice a day. Compliance is very important to achieve control of the pain and inflammation associated with RA. The important factors include:

1. A simple dosing schedule, this is the most important factor in achieving compliance.
2. Belief in health care.

    A belief in the benefits of health care and confidence in your physician's ability is essential to compliance with therapy.
3. Doctor's instructions.

    Busy doctors may not always provide patients with complete instructions about medications. The miscommunication may lead to improper use of medications. Ask your doctor for written instructions on how to take your medication properly.
4. Beliefs about drugs.

    Many patients believe that NSAIDs are interchangeable, and may even take the NSAIDs prescribed for other family members or friends NSAIDs, or add an over-the-counter medication without consulting their doctors. These mistakes may lead to a much higher chance of developing side effects.

Simplicity is the key to compliance. Compliance is the key to effectiveness.

T = Tolerability

An NSAID must be well tolerated if it is to be taken regularly. If a particular NSAID upsets your stomach, makes you feel weak, gives you a headache, or changes your bowel habits, ask for another drug right away. The tolerability of NSAIDs can be improved by taking the prescribed dose on a full stomach, and by avoiding alcohol and caffeine. Taking NSAIDs on an empty stomach, or with alcohol or caffeine can increase your chance of developing stomach ulcers.

A = Adverse Reactions (Side Effects)

During the past 20 years, the safety of NSAIDs has been frequently discussed. Nonsteroidal anti-inflammatory drugs make up 5% of all drugs used but 25% of all side effects caused. The side effects can be serious, but in most patients, the risks associated with these side effects are outweighed by the clear benefits of controlling arthritis. Remember that uncontrolled arthritis has serious side effects too. The major side effects of NSAIDs are shown in Table 5–1.

1. Effects on the gastrointestinal tract.
    Nonsteroidal anti-inflammatory drugs can injure the gastrointestinal tract, most commonly by decreasing prostaglandin synthesis, which damages the protective lining of the stomach. All NSAIDs can damage the

Table 5–1: Major Side Effects (Adverse Reactions) of NSAIDs
Adverse Reactions
GI damage
Renal damage
Liver damage
Asthma
Blood cell actions
Skin rashes

gastrointestinal tract. This damage can be as mild as irritation, or as serious as ulceration, massive bleeding, or even death. Although the chances of damage are higher with nausea, stomach damage or even an ulcer can also occur with no warning symptoms. Patients with high risk of developing NSAID stomach toxicity include patients over 65; patients with previous stomach problems or ulcers; and patients who smoke, drink alcohol, take steroids, or have conditions that might also damage the stomach (Table 5–2).

Misoprostol, or Cytotec, is a medication which, when given with NSAIDs, protects the stomach and prevents NSAID damage.

2. Effects on kidney function.

Nonsteroidal anti–inflammatory drugs also affect normal kidney function. They may cause fluid retention or

Table 5–2: High-Risk Factors for Ulcers with NSAIDs
1. Age
>60, especially >70
2. History of ulcers
G.I. Intolerance
3. Other diseases
Heart
Cancer
4. Drugs
Alcohol
Tobacco
Steroids

an increase in blood pressure. In order to make the safest treatment choices, if you have kidney disease or high blood pressure, talk to your doctor before taking NSAIDs.

3. Effects on liver function.

Occasionally NSAIDs may cause liver damage, particularly Sulindac (Clinoril) and Voltaren (Diclofenac). After a month of therapy with these drugs, have your blood tested to make sure liver damage is not occurring.

4. Effects in asthmatic patients.

Some patients with asthma may have a sensitivity to ASA and other NSAIDs. This sensitivity can lead to severe asthma within 1 hour of taking an NSAID. If you have a sensitivity to ASA or other NSAIDs, let your doctor know. It is possible to desensitize you by starting with a low NSAID dose and gradually increasing it.

5. Effects of blood clotting.

ASA and other NSAIDs inhibit blood clotting. Although ASA is often prescribed to prevent heart attacks or strokes it can lead to increased bruising. When other drugs that affect clotting are prescribed in addition to ASA, bleeding can result. Talk to your doctor and pharmacist about all the drugs you are taking, so that no negative drug interactions occur.

R = Relative Efficacy

All NSAIDs control inflammation and relieve pain. However, they do not stop major disease progression. Nonsteroidal anti-inflammatory drugs affect prostaglandins differently; benefits vary for different patients, doses, and NSAIDs. Certain NSAIDs in the STAR$ group are more effective in most patients and, therefore, in my opinion, should be used first.

Over time, the initial effectiveness of an NSAID may wane. Substituting a different NSAID STAR$ will usually solve the problem.

$ = Cost

Compared to ASA, newer NSAIDs are expensive, usually due to the cost of developing new drugs and testing them before they are approved for use. Although the cost of NSAIDs is important, the more important cost to consider is the real overall cost of uncontrolled RA: Costs to society of disability, unemployment, and adverse reactions.

The choice of an NSAID is a decision made between you and your doctor; it can usually be made relatively quickly. Most doctors use a group of NSAIDs regularly. They are familiar with each drug's efficacy and side effects. The following NSAID STAR$ have excellent profiles, and should be the first drugs that you choose, not the last. In my view, the current NSAID STAR$ are the following:

- Arthrotec/Voltaren
- Disalcid
- Naproxen
- Relafen
- Surgam
- Ultradol

SUMMARY

Nonsteroidal anti-inflammatory drugs remain the backbone of therapy for RA. NSAID STAR$ have the best overall profile, and in my opinion, should be used first in full effective doses. Although NSAIDs relieve inflammation and pain, they do not prevent disease progression. Nonsteroidal anti-inflammatory drugs are used alone only in mild, non-progressive disease.

COMMON MISTAKES

1. Not taking a full therapeutic dose.
   Full doses are needed for efficacy.
2. Not taking misoprostol.
   Gastrointestinal side effects are the most common problem with NSAIDs. If you are over 65, have had ulcers, are taking other drugs that may cause ulcers, or have other diseases that may damage your stomach, I recommend misoprostol (Cytotec).

COMMON QUESTIONS

Q: Why can I not take ASA? It is much cheaper than the NSAID STAR$.

A: ASA certainly works, but effective treatment with ASA requires 10 to 12 pills daily and carries a greater risk of ulcers.

Q: Can I take other drugs with my NSAID?

A: Although some medications do not cause problems when taken with NSAIDs, others do. Always check with your doctor and your pharmacist.

Q: Can I take anticoagulants with my NSAID?

A: It depends on the situation—discuss the combination with your physician.

Q: My stomach does not hurt—am I safe from stomach problems?

A: No. Most ulcers cause no pain. You find out you have an ulcer when you bleed. This is another reason to use the safest NSAIDs and misoprostol if you are at high risk of stomach problems.

Q: What other NSAIDs are available?

A: Ansaid (flurbiprofen)
Clinoril (sulindac)
Entrophen (ASA)
Feldene (piroxicam)
Indocid (indomethacin)
Mobiflex (tenoxicam)
Motrin (ibuprofen)
Nalfon (fenoprofen)
Nova-butazone (Phenylbutazone)

CHAPTER SIX

DMARDs: DISEASE-MODIFYING ANTIRHEUMATIC DRUGS, THE FOUNDATION OF TREATMENT

Disease-modifying antirheumatic drugs (DMARDs) are a group of drugs with a proven ability to slow the course of rheumatoid arthritis and limit progression of the disease in the joints. Unfortunately, because of their side effects, and their higher position in the classical treatment pyramid, both patients and doctors frequently shy away from using DMARDs. These are often used too late, at the wrong doses, and with complicated monitoring regimens. This delay means lost opportunity to gain control of rheumatoid arthritis early in the disease.

Joint damage in rheumatoid arthritis usually occurs in the early stages of the disease. It is important to stop the disease process and limit joint damage as quickly as possible. Nonsteroidal anti-inflammatory drugs alone do not prevent damage. It is essential to use DMARDs early in RA.

BASIC CHARACTERISTICS OF DMARDs

The basic characteristics of DMARDs follow:

- Effective in controlling progression of RA
- Have a mechanism of action that is unknown
- Require a long time to build up on effect
- Require monitoring for significant adverse reactions
- Have benefits that may diminish over time

In some patients, DMARD combinations are more effective, and response to one drug does not predict response to another.

CONTROLLING DISEASE PROGRESSION

All DMARDs control rheumatoid arthritis, at least for a while, and often permanently. They appear to turn off the inflammatory process, reduce pain and swelling, and stop the damage caused by RA.

MECHANISM OF ACTION

The mechanism of action of DMARDs is not fully understood. Although we know that DMARDs affect cells, their interactions, and what chemicals they release, we do not fully know. However, we do know that, in RA, DMARDs work!

TIME REQUIRED FOR EFFECT

DMARDs take several weeks to a few months to turn off the inflammatory process. The three major DMARDs are methotrexate, hydroxychloroquine (Plaquenil), and gold. Methotrexate may be effective in 6 to 12 weeks, whereas hydroxychloroquine and gold may take from 3-6 months. This lack of immediate, or even quick, benefit is clearly a problem with DMARDs. Taking DMARDs is like beginning to exercise, cutting back on calories, or trying to stop smoking; you must be confident that the benefits will eventually become obvious. Unfortunately, a DMARD that works immediately does not yet exist.

ADVERSE REACTIONS

Each DMARD has specific and significant side effects, including organ damage and even death. For example, gold can suppress the activity of the bone marrow, methotrexate can cause liver and lung damage, and hydroxychloroquine can produce vision disturbances. Sulfasalazine can affect the blood.

The risks of these drugs are, however, less than the benefits of controlling RA. All of these drugs are prescribed in low doses for rheumatoid arthritis and, therefore, are relatively safe to use. The adverse reactions are minor compared to progression of RA. The side effects of DMARDs can be limited by careful monitoring; in fact, most adverse reactions of DMARDs are minor and reversible. These drugs are moderately expensive and require regular doctor visits and occasional blood tests.

PRINCIPLES FOR USING DMARDs

1. Use DMARDs as soon as possible, especially in early RA.

   Using DMARDs in early RA takes advantage of an important window of opportunity to prevent joint damage. Delays in controlling RA with a DMARD often mean more serious long-term consequences. It is, however, better to use a DMARD late in the disease, than not at all.

2. Develop an appropriate monitoring schedule.

   You and your doctor must set up an acceptable monitoring program. Normally, monitoring programs can be simplified, to allow you to live a normal life while ensuring safe therapy. Although your monitoring program can be made more acceptable, DMARDs do need continuous monitoring; it is very important that you stay with the agreed-upon monitoring program.

3. Choose the right DMARD and dose.

   The choice and dose of a DMARD vary, depending on the patient and the temperament of the disease. Because DMARDs work by different mechanisms and can affect different organ systems, you and your doctor should discuss which DMARD would be best for you: The effectiveness and side effects of DMARDs differ, depending on the patient, the dose, and the severity of the disease.

4. DMARDs are a flexible therapy.

    In general, DMARDs are used selectively for different patients and temperaments of RA. As you can see, in the second ring of the treatment target (Figure 4–1), hydroxychloroquine and sulfasalazine are often the drugs used first in patients with mild disease. Methotrexate and gold, because of their increased effectiveness, are used in patients with moderate and severe disease. In patients who have severe or uncontrolled disease, combinations of DMARDs shown in the third ring, are used first.

5. Diminishing effects over time.

    The benefits of DMARDs may diminish over time; if a decrease in benefits occurs, it is usually after several years or even decades of successful therapy. Methotrexate, the most long-acting DMARD, often controls RA for over 20 years. The benefits of gold and hydroxychloroquine tend to decrease sooner; sulfasalazine is the earliest to lose its benefits.

6. Lack of effectiveness or adverse reactions with one DMARD does not predict response to another.

    All DMARDs are different. Lack of effectiveness or side effects experienced with one drug does not predict response to another. If you are to achieve control of RA, it is important that you and your doctor select another drug as soon as it is clear that the first choice is not suitable. An alternative to switching drugs is adding a second DMARD, if your RA is incompletely controlled.

RECOMMENDED FIRST LEVEL DMARDs

In my opinion, the DMARDs described below are the recommended DMARDs.

Methotrexate

Methotrexate is the leading DMARD used in North
America. Methotrexate is effective within 6 to 12 weeks for
most patients. Monitoring and controlling adverse reactions
are relatively simple. Methotrexate is often combined with
other drugs, and its benefits rarely diminish over time.
Methotrexate is normally prescribed at a starting dose of 2 to
4 pills per week (5 to 10 mg). The dose can easily be individualized, with lower doses for smaller, older patients, and
higher doses for younger, healthier, larger patients. The starting dose is then increased, up to 6 to 8 pills per week,
depending on the course of the disease. Blood tests alert
your doctor to the development of side effects. When RA is
controlled, the dose can sometimes be reduced to a lower
long-term maintenance dose, usually a few pills per week.

Most patients respond well to methotrexate; between
50% and 80% of patients achieve effective control of RA.
Because absorption of the pills varies among patients, when
benefit is incomplete, methotrexate may be given weekly by
injection.

Methotrexate: Side Effects.   The most common problems with methotrexate are nausea, heartburn, inflammation
in the mouth, and hair loss. Normally the side effects can be
reversed, either by decreasing the dose of methotrexate if the
disease is under control, or by adding a vitamin pill contain-
ing folic or folinic acid, 12 to 18 hours after the methotrexate dose. Although your doctor may prefer to wait until side
effects occur, I prefer to add 5 mg of folic acid, 5 days a

week, to the methotrexate regimen from the beginning. It is better to prevent side effects than to treat them.

More serious, but uncommon, problems with methotrexate include inflammation and scarring in the liver or the lungs. Most patients who develop liver problems with methotrexate have underlying medical conditions that make them susceptible to this side effect: diabetes, alcoholism, liver disease, hepatitis, or obesity. When patients with liver disease require methotrexate, liver biopsies can ensure that no additional damage is taking place. Inflammation and scarring in the lungs results from hypersensitivity to the drug, and occurs relatively early in the course of treatment. Most patients with lung problems notice increased shortness of breath and often a dry cough. Mention these problems to your physician if they occur.

When taking methotrexate it is important that you discuss other drugs you are taking with your doctor or pharmacist to ensure that no serious interaction occurs. Drugs such as co-trimoxazole (Septra, Bactrim) must be avoided, because they influence how methotrexate is broken down in the body.

Methotrexate can also suppress the bone marrow, decreasing the numbers of platelets, white blood cells, or red blood cells. Your doctor may do periodic blood tests to ensure this is not happening.

Methotrexate: Cost and Convenience. Methotrexate is relatively inexpensive. Because it only needs to be monitored every few weeks to every few months, and because it is given in one oral dose or one injection per week, it is convenient. As a result of its effectiveness, low cost, and convenience, methotrexate has become the most important drug in the treatment of rheumatoid arthritis.

Hydroxychloroquine (Plaquenil)

Hydroxychloroquine (Plaquenil) has been used since the early 1950s to treat rheumatoid arthritis. Initially, a related drug, chloroquine, was used, but chloroquine had more serious side-effects. Because of the higher incidence of side effects with chloroquine, both drugs fell out of favor. Recently, studies have shown that hydroxychloroquine is more effective and much safer than chloroquine.

The mechanism of action of hydroxychloroquine is unknown; the time required for response may be 3 to 6 months. Monitoring involves yearly eye examinations. Hydroxychloroquine (Plaquenil) can be used in combination with methotrexate or sulfasalazine. It is useful in patients with moderate and severe RA.

The dose of hydroxychloroquine (Plaquenil) is one or two pills (200 mg) taken at bedtime. Patients may experience nausea, but other side effects are very uncommon. During the first few months of treatment, you may not notice much improvement, but the severity of rheumatoid arthritis gradually decreases.

Hydroxychloroquine (Plaquenil) is an inexpensive, safe, easily monitored DMARD that works well in early and mild RA. In combination with other DMARDs, plaquenil is useful for more severe disease temperaments.

Injectable Gold

Gold was the first DMARD. In the 1920s, gold was found to control tuberculosis. Gold was then tried in rheumatoid arthritis because it was thought that the disease was caused by an infectious agent. Although gold clearly does work in controlling rheumatoid arthritis, its mechanism of action is still unknown. Gold normally takes 4 to 6 months to work. The cost of monitoring is high, and gold causes many adverse reactions. The benefits of gold diminish with time, usually in a time frame somewhere between that of hydroxychloroquine and methotrexate. When gold works, the response is dramatic. Gold is one of the few drugs that appears to bring about a complete remission of the disease that can last for years. In patients with only partial improvement, the effect of gold decreases earlier.

Approximately 30% of patients taking gold experience side effects. Most side effects are mild and common; they include an itchy skin rash, protein in the urine, and inflammation of the mouth. A more severe side effect is kidney damage (nephrotic syndrome), seen in 5% of patients. This can occur within the first 6 months of treatment.

The most serious side effect of gold is suppression of the bone marrow, probably due to a hypersensitivity reaction. This marrow suppression can result in a decreased number of blood clotting cells, or platelets (thrombocytopenia), a decreased number of white cells (neutropenia), or an absence of all types of cells (bone marrow failure, or aplasia). Bone marrow suppression is the most serious and feared side effect of gold treatment; it is the main reason the drug is prescribed much less frequently than methotrexate. However, when the side effects of gold are compared to the side effects of rheumatoid arthritis, the benefits of gold clearly outweigh the risks. Before using gold as a therapy for rheumatoid arthritis, you should discuss all the relative benefits and risks with your doctor.

Gold: Cost and Convenience. Unfortunately, gold is both expensive and inconvenient. Weekly gold injections, blood tests, and urine tests are costly. Despite its side effects, cost, and inconvenience, gold remains a useful drug. In patients with only partial improvement, gold may be combined with another DMARD such as cyclosporine.

Sulfasalazine

Sulfasalazine has been widely used in RA only during the past 10 years. Although its mechanism of action is unknown, studies have shown that it controls RA. Sulfasalazine begins working after 4 to 12 weeks of therapy, faster than gold or hydroxychloroquine. It is also well tolerated; the most frequent side effects are gastrointestinal pain, nausea, malaise, dizziness, and headache. However, allergic skin rashes and a decrease in all blood cells do occur. Most side effects occur within the first 3 months of treatment.

Sulfasalazine is usually taken as a daily dose of 2 to 3 grams. Ideally the dose is increased slowly: 500 mg daily during week 1; 1000 mg daily during week 2; 1500 mg daily during week 3; and 2 grams daily during week 4. Blood tests should be scheduled monthly for the first 3 months, then every 3 months. In some cases, sulfasalazine has been combined successfully with methotrexate and hydroxychloroquine. Since sulfasalazine may interact with other drugs, review your other medications with your doctor. Sulfasalazine is a fast-acting, moderately effective, less toxic DMARD; its beneficial effects may decrease more rapidly than other DMARDs.

SECOND LEVEL DMARDs:

Combination DMARDs

During the past 20 years, DMARDs have often been combined with steroids and anti-inflammatory drugs. However, recent studies in patients with early, rheumatoid arthritis have shown that combining *lower doses of several* DMARDs may be better than using a higher dose of only one DMARD. Currently, evidence suggests that methotrexate combined with hydroxychloroquine and/or sulfasalazine or cyclosporine may be effective for people whose arthritis does not respond to one drug alone. Research is in progress to determine which combinations of DMARDs are effective in patients with different types of RA (Figure 4–1). I believe that combination DMARDs are the recommended option in RA with a severe temperament.

THIRD LEVEL DMARDs:
Experimental or Older Dmards

Experimental Disease-Modifying Drugs

Over the past 5 years, many new immunologic or biologic treatments have been developed to control rheumatoid arthritis. These affect specific mediators or chemicals involved in the inflammatory process. To date, the role of these treatments is unclear. They are currently used in patients with severe and unresponsive disease. Clinical trials are underway to compare these drugs with currently available DMARDs. Within 5 years, we should know whether any of these drugs should become a first- or second-level DMARD.

Older DMARDs

Some older DMARDs are declining in usefulness and have been relegated to the third-level. They simply cannot compete with the recommended, or first-level, DMARDs. Others are not yet well tested and, therefore, are not as widely used. These drugs include D-penicillamine, oral gold, cyclosporine, azathioprine, cyclophosphamide, and tetracycline. Cyclosporine A has recently been reintroduced as Neoral. This drug works well especially in early RA or in combination with methotrexate or gold. Cyclosporine A in this new form may become a first level DMARD.

RESEARCH

Critical research in rheumatoid arthritis is being undertaken worldwide by interested rheumatologists and scientists, often supported by national arthritis societies. These organizations are funded by your donations; they have a major role in initiating and coordinating drug treatment research in many countries. This research has markedly changed the management of rheumatoid arthritis over the past 20 years. Patients who would have been hospitalized because of severe disease can now often be treated as outpatients. Arthritis and rheumatism societies have been instrumental in improving patient care, linking the public and health care teams, setting national standards for education, and initiating and coordinating research in arthritis. Cooperation between these various groups has led to a better outcome than could be achieved by any one group alone.

SUMMARY

Disease-modifying antirheumatic drugs are the foundation of the treatment of rheumatoid arthritis. When used early in the disease, and over the long-term, DMARDs can control RA and slow or prevent disease progression. Unfortunately DMARDs are often considered to be second-choice drugs that require too much monitoring. However, in most patients these drugs can be both effective and safe. We need more safe and effective DMARDs. The recommended DMARDs, methotrexate, hydroxychloroquine (Plaquenil), and gold, are simply not enough. What if one is contraindicated, another causes side effects, and the last one you tried is not effective? Few real options beyond combinations are available. Many patients who still have progressive disease need new effective DMARDs to control their RA.

COMMON MISTAKES

1. Delay.

   Rheumatoid arthritis patients may delay DMARD therapy for months or years for many reasons: hope for a spontaneous remission, stress, or even family planning. Almost all of these patients wish that they had started a DMARD sooner.

2. Taking a low dose.

   Some people start a DMARD, but take the lowest dose possible. The difference in side effects between a low and therapeutic dose is minimal, the difference in benefit is remarkable. Take the dose that does the job.

3. Stopping too soon.

   Unfortunately, DMARDs take a long time to work. Even though you may notice no improvement during the first few weeks or even months it is important to persist until the DMARD has time to work.

COMMON QUESTIONS

Q: Which DMARD should I take?

A: Everyone is unique. The choice of DMARD should be discussed by you and your doctor. Most DMARDs that are used first are the ones that I recommend: methotrexate, hydroxychloroquine, gold, and occasionally sulfasalazine. The dose depends on the stage and severity of your disease, potential benefits, and side effects. Some general principles apply:

   1. Mild disease: Hydroxychloroquine or sulfasalazine.
      Moderate disease: Methotrexate or gold.
      Severe disease: DMARD combination.
   2. Fast response required: Methotrexate.
   3. Problem with frequent injections or blood tests:

Hydroxychloroquine or methotrexate.

4. Liver problems: Methotrexate may be avoided.
    Kidney problems: Gold may be avoided.

Q: What happens if I experience side effects?

A: Some DMARD side effects can be easily resolved, but others may require stopping the drug. If the drug cannot be restarted, another DMARD may be tried. Most side effects are treatable and will resolve. However, severe side effects, and sometimes even death, may occasionally occur. In general, taking a DMARD is safer than leaving the disease uncontrolled.

Q: Does gold really have gold in it?

A: Yes. Although we do not know why, it is the gold that affects RA.

Q: Should I wait for a new DMARD to be available before I start treatment?

A: No. Delay means joint damage. Start a DMARD now: If the perfect DMARD comes along, you can always change. A DMARD will not reverse the damage that has already been done, but will still help control the disease.

Q: Can I try an older DMARD before a combination?

A: Many patients do, and usually this does not work. In my view, a proven combination has a much better chance of providing effective treatment now.

A SECOND OPINION

Dr Bensen is absolutely right to point out that a lot can be done to get RA under control! Interestingly, our treatment modalities have not changed very much in the past 10 to 20 years. However we have learned to use what is available in a more intelligent way.

Take, for example, steroids. When they were discovered in the early 50s, many thought that a cure had been found for rheumatoid arthritis. However their popularity was to be short lived. It was soon realized that high doses taken on a continuous basis for prolonged periods of time was associated with significant side effects. When I became a rheumatologist in the early eighties, it was almost considered malpractice to use them. Fortunately, we have now realized that steroids can be, not only extremely helpful, but also safe when used appropriately. I "confess" that I use low dose steroids in all my patients with moderate and severe arthritis when I start them on DMARDs. The logic behind this approach is quite simple: It is crucial to control the inflammation as quickly as possible. Since DMARDs take a minimum of 6 weeks to start working, steroids can do the job for them until the DMARDs take over. I make a "contract" with my patients and give them prednisone 10 mg in the morning for 2 weeks, and decrease the dosage by 2.5 mg every 2 weeks. Since steroids are by far the best anti–inflammatory drug available, most can even stop their NSAIDs. With this protocol, 60 percent of my patients have been able to stop the prednisone after 2 months and 40 percent have required a second 2-month "contract". None has remained on it beyond 4 months! I much prefer this approach to giving higher doses (20 or 30 mg) for shorter periods of time, because I would be afraid that some patients might feel "too well" and be reluctant to stop the drug completely. The temptation would then be to leave them on a low dosage, 5 to 7.5 mg daily, which I prefer to avoid.

I will make another important point about intra-articular steroids: Make sure that you completely rest the joint for at least 1, preferably 2, days after the injection. This is particularily important for weight-bearing joints such as the knee, hip, or ankle. If you do so you will see a significant increase in the duration of efficacy of the injection.

One of the most important messages delivered by Dr Bensen is that rheumatoid arthritis can be an aggressive disease and that an aggressive disease needs aggressive remedies, now, not down the line, but at the front of the line. I couldn't agree with him more .

How can you know that you are affected by severe, rather than mild, disease? It should be quite easy. The higher the number of painful and swollen joints you have, the longer the duration of your stiffness in the morning and the higher the degree of your limitations, the more likely you are to be affected by severe disease. Don't be reassured by a normal, or only slightly, elevated sedimentation rate. If you have the above symptoms, the ESR does not always correlate with the degree of inflammation in the joints. With your doctor and the other members of your health care team, make sure that specific strategies are planned to address all of your needs. So much can be done! Nowadays, most, if not all, patients can win the battle against rheumatoid arthritis. So can you.

Simon Carette M.D., F.R.C.P.C.
Professor of Medicine
Head, Department of Medicine
Le Centre Hospitalier de l'Université Laval
Centre Hospitalier Universitaire du Québec

Steroids have an important role in managing rheumatoid arthritis (RA). Steroids or corticosteroids include cortisone and its synthetic derivatives. Steroids are hormones; your adrenal glands secrete steroids. Cortisone was the first steroid, and was produced in the early 1950s. Since then, synthetic derivatives, with greater potency and fewer side effects than cortisone, have been developed. These include prednisone, an oral steroid, and methylprednisolone and triamcinolone, injectable steroids. Because cortisone had a remarkable effect on inflammatory conditions, its use became popular in the early 1950s. Also, because "more" was considered "better," many arthritis patients took high doses of cortisone for long periods of time. Although their arthritis improved temporarily, these patients developed severe side effects. As a result, steroids were often not used in the '70s and '80s. Now steroids are being prescribed in the lowest dose that controls inflammation in order to keep adverse reactions to a minimum. Steroids can be given orally or by injection into the joint, into a muscle, or into a vein.

ORAL STEROIDS

Oral steroids are frequently used in rheumatoid arthritis. A short course of prednisone (15 mg, tapering down to 5 mg in 5-day intervals) will usually control the early or flared RA and allow you to resume more normal activities. Sometimes, higher doses are needed, due to individual differences in response. Short courses of steroids quickly control RA and cause few steroid side effects. Some patients with uncontrolled, severe, and progressive rheumatoid arthritis will decide to take steroids on a daily basis, recognizing that they will have some side effects in 5 to 10 years. Low doses of prednisone (between 5 and 10 mg), minimize side effects yet allow patients to live a more normal life, with their inflammation controlled. Many patients with severe arthritis know that a normal life would be impossible without these potent drugs.

INTRA-ARTICULAR STEROIDS

Some steroids can be injected directly into an inflamed joint. Although this procedure has a reputation for being painful, with the new thin needles, and an experienced doctor, you will barely feel most injections. Normally, 20 to 40 mg of methylprednisolone or triamcinolone are injected into a large joint, and 10 to 20 mg of drug are injected into a small joint. Steroids injected into a joint often stop inflammation almost immediately, and the effect may last for a few months. Within the first day or two after a steroid injection, some of the steroid moves from the joint into the blood, making you feel generally better all over. The intra-articular approach is preferable if only a few joints are inflamed, if oral steroids are not easily tolerated, or if other diseases such as diabetes or glaucoma are present.

INTRAMUSCULAR STEROIDS

Intramuscular injections of steroids give the same anti-inflammatory effect as an oral dose, but cause fewer side effects. Forty to 80 mg can be injected when RA is diagnosed to control inflammation until NSAIDs and DMARDs take effect.

INTRAVENOUS STEROIDS

Two to three large (500 to 1000 mg) doses of steroids, injected into a vein over a 1-week period, will often rapidly check uncontrolled RA. The benefits of this aggressive approach can last a few weeks or a few months. Intravenous steroids are also used to slow disease progression when a severe flare-up has occurred, and the patient cannot rest or use other drugs. Often, oral or intramuscular steroids work as well as intravenous and should be tried first.

Side effects of intravenous steroids include flushing, headache, and skin rash. Rarely, steroids can cause bone damage or gastrointestinal problems.

At one time, rheumatology patients were hospitalized for many months for bed rest, their joints in splints, to try to wait until the disease could be brought under control with drugs. This had a huge social and financial cost for the patient, his or her family, and the health care system. With the renewed use of steroids and better control of RA with DMARDs, this has now changed. Small inexpensive doses can produce the same effect as months of hospital bed rest, and better still, allow you to continue a more normal lifestyle.

ADVERSE REACTIONS

Steroids can cause important adverse reactions, which are related to the specific steroid, the individual, the dose, and the duration of therapy. Susceptible patients who take steroids at high doses, over a long period of time, will have the most severe adverse reactions.

1. Weight gain

    Steroids may increase appetite, resulting in weight gain. You may notice changes in your skin, with an increase in bruising, or even stretch marks. Your doctor can minimize these changes by lowering the dose, using them on alternate days, or injecting them into joints. In some patients, the benefits of steroids cannot be separated from a frustrating weight gain.

2. Osteoporosis

   Osteoporosis, the thinning of bones that increases the risk of fracture, is a problem in RA. Loss of bone is worsened by steroids, even if taken only for short periods of time. Steroids increase calcium loss, leading to decreased calcium in the bones. Decreased bone mass results in increasing bone fragility, resulting in compression fractures in the spine, and in other bones. The most effective ways of minimizing steroid-induced osteoporosis include low doses and short duration of use. Giving the drug intramuscularly or intra-articularly, and oral steroids with calcium and vitamin D, or with other bone-preserving drugs to prevent development of osteoporosis, is usually helpful.

3. The eye

   Steroids appear to stimulate the formation of cataracts. Once cataract formation has begun, it tends to continue even after steroids are stopped. Cataract formation also increases with age and with long-term exposure to sunlight. To minimize the risk of cataract formation with steroids, the dose should be as low as possible. Steroids can also affect glaucoma, a condition in which the fluid pressure in the eye increases, damaging the retina and affecting vision. If you experience increasing pain in your eye(s) while taking steroids, you should call your physician. If you have glaucoma, be sure to talk with your ophthalmologist before taking steroids, so that preventative measures can be initiated.

4. Heart and blood vessel disease

   Steroids can worsen high blood pressure or high cholesterol, leading to premature heart disease and stroke.

5. Diabetes mellitus

   Steroids increase blood sugar levels. Although this effect is usually short lived, if you are "prediabetic," your blood sugar may rise into a range usually seen only in diabetes. In early diabetes, steroids will increase blood sugar and make the antidiabetic drugs seem ineffective. If you take insulin, steroids will elevate blood sugar; you may need to increase the insulin dose.

SUMMARY

For the past 45 years, steroids have provided effective anti-inflammatory therapy in rheumatoid arthritis. To minimize side effects, steroids are best prescribed in the lowest possible doses for the shortest possible period of time. They can be used orally or by injection. Steroids remain a significant part of *combination* drug therapy in rheumatoid arthritis. Steroids are the best anti-inflammatory drugs available, but they may also limit disease progression.

COMMON MISTAKES

1. Not taking steroids when you need them.
    Many patients feel that steroids are dangerous.
    Appropriately used, steroids make a real difference to how you feel, and to your arthritis.
2. Refusing injectable steroids because you fear the pain.
    Steroid injections, done properly by an experienced doctor, are rarely painful.

COMMON QUESTIONS

Q: Will I gain weight if I take prednisone?
A: Maybe. Usually, low-dose oral, intramuscular or intra-articular steroids do not cause weight gain. High-dose oral or intravenous steroids usually do cause weight gain.
Q: I have osteoporosis. Will steroids make it worse?

A: Yes. Untreated RA with disability also makes osteoporosis worse. The osteoporosis-promoting effects of steroids can normally be stopped by adding calcium, vitamin D (halibut oil), or a specific anti-osteoporosis drug.

Q: People tell me if I start steroids I will never get off. Is this true?

A: Not usually. Most patients can discontinue steroids to an acceptable dose once inflammation is controlled.

A SECOND OPINION

Steroids are important treatment options for physicians caring for patients with rheumatoid arthritis, particularly when their disease needs to be controlled. Unfortunately, as with all good medicines, there are potential adverse effects such as osteoporosis. High doses of steroids inevitably lead to bone loss and osteoporosis. Low doses (less than 7.5 mg/day of prednisone) may not be as deleterious; however, many physicians feel that there is no safe dose to prevent bone loss. Recent advances in our understanding of steroid-induced osteoporosis may have overcome this problem. Studies have shown that hormone replacement therapy (HRT) is of benefit in menopausal women with rheumatoid arthritis for those on or off steroids. With HRT, increases in bone mass, and therefore bone strength, have been seen. HRT is also beneficial in the treatment and prevention of heart disease and possibly stroke. For those who do not tolerate HRT, the bisphosphonates are good alternatives. Studies using cyclic etidronate, pamidronate and alendronate have proven effective in the prevention and treatment of bone loss.

J.D. Adachi, M.D., F.R.C.P.C.
Professor of Medicine
McMaster University
Director, Rheumatoid Disease Unit
St. Joseph's Hospital

CHAPTER EIGHT

YOUR HEALTH CARE TEAM

Patients with rheumatoid arthritis (RA), especially those with moderate and severe disease, benefit from the care of various health professionals. Their skills can make a real difference in your arthritis and in your daily life. This team of professionals focuses on helping you to do the things that you like, want, or need to do. In order to derive the maximum benefit from these health care practitioners, you must understand the role of each member of your team. You must also see yourself as the team captain and use your team wisely. This chapter outlines the roles of some of these health care professionals.

PHYSIOTHERAPISTS

Physiotherapists can help to reduce joint inflammation by using passive heat and cold. Your physiotherapist may use one, or both, of these methods to decrease pain and swelling. In addition, physiotherapists teach exercises to strengthen the muscles which allow you to support your joints without causing any joint damage. Physiotherapists can advise you on using conservative nonmedicinal methods to reduce the swelling in inflamed joints, including positioning and rest. Correct posture, a regular fitness program, and pool therapy may also lessen the stress of RA on joints. Physiotherapists often work with occupational therapists to reduce inflammation, increase function, and prevent joint damage.

OCCUPATIONAL THERAPISTS

Occupational therapists work with you in different ways. These professionals can assist you in protecting your joints, by making splints for both work and rest and by making insoles for your shoes. In addition, they can advise you on aids for your home or your workplace that will help you to do the tasks that you want to do and, at the same time, protect your joints. Occupational therapists can teach techniques that will help you in your daily life, including correct patterns of movement, daily exercise, and energy conservation.

NURSES

Nurses trained in arthritic diseases have many important roles. Nurses provide support and education about medical problems and treatments; they may also coordinate your individualized treatment plan. Nurses may recommend the involvement of other health professionals to help you improve function and cope with other problems associated with arthritis. In our view, they do not participate enough in the management of RA, where we have "too few doing too little for too many."

SOCIAL WORKERS

Social workers have the expertise to help with many personal problems frequently associated with RA. Patients with RA often have problems adjusting to changes in their roles both inside and outside the home, in lifestyle, and in relationships. Depression, anger, marital or sexual problems, or problems with children, money, or your job can become overwhelming when you are also faced with the added stress and fatigue of a chronic disease. Social workers can provide insight, counseling, and referral to community resources to help you cope with, or solve these problems. In addition, social workers will often form, or refer you to support groups where several people with arthritis can share their stories, problems, and solutions.

PHARMACISTS

Pharmacists are the experts on drugs—still the most significant form of therapy for RA. Pharmacists can teach you and the team about the problems to avoid in RA. If you have any problems, write down your symptoms and bring the note with you to your next appointment. Remember to take your medications as they have been prescribed. The pharmacist will provide you with helpful hints for remembering your medicine and also for managing minor side effects of medications.

NUTRITIONISTS

Good nutrition, including a balanced diet, appropriate weight, and management of any nutritional problems is important in RA. Eating sensibly helps to ensure that you stay in good general health. Although diet alone will not directly influence RA, a healthy diet can make other treatments, especially medications, work better. If weight loss is a goal, the nutritionist can develop a diet especially for you. Most patients with RA have preferences in their diets. Some find that certain foods make their arthritis worse. It is best to avoid these foods. Others find that taking vitamins makes their arthritis better. These can be continued.

In RA many vitamins or folk medicines have never been tested; as long as they do not harm you they can be tried. However, scientifically proven medication should not be ignored or stopped. Usually the two approaches can be taken together.

COMMUNITY AND SELF-HELP GROUPS

Support groups that share an interest in arthritic diseases, especially RA, are made up of arthritis patients, family members, and often, interested health professionals. These groups can help you learn more about your arthritis and solve the day-to-day problems of living with arthritis. Some people become involved for both social and educational purposes. These groups also act as advocates, informing society, health professionals and government about the needs of patients with arthritis.

THE PATIENT

The negative effects of RA on your life can often be limited by setting realistic goals and by getting help when you need it. Realistic personal, spousal, family, and work goals are essential when you have arthritis. Stress can cause flare-ups in arthritis, which causes more stress and worsens the situation. Balance is the key. The support of your spouse, children, family, and colleagues is very important. You must clearly state what you can do and stick with it. Often, a member of your health care team, a support group member, or even a friend can share their experiences and help you to cope with the problems of life with arthritis.

You are the captain of your health care team. Make sure your needs are met. You make the choices about your therapy and about the role of the members of your health care team in your treatment.

SUMMARY

In addition to drug therapy, the health care team provides important services and support for all patients with RA. Its expertise is essential for patients with moderate and severe RA.

This chapter was jointly developed with Beth Snowden, R.N., and Nurse Education in Rheumatic Diseases.

CHAPTER NINE

CONQUERING YOUR RHEUMATOID ARTHRITIS: PUTTING THE PIECES TOGETHER

In this chapter, the information presented throughout the book is pulled together. First we discuss the principles of treatment. Next, we focus on the selective treatment available for the different categories of RA. The specifics of this overview will vary for each patient so that, for the best treatment choices to be made, you must communicate your needs and fears to your doctor.

PRINCIPLES FOR TREATING RHEUMATOID ARTHRITIS

The basic principles for managing your RA follow. (Think of the acronym "ESAP" [Early, Selective, Aggressive, Persistent], "ASAP."

Early—Treat as early as possible
Like a fire, if the inflammation of rheumatoid arthritis spreads, it causes damage. Inflammation can cause damage to cartilage, bone, or other tissues within the first few months of onset of the disease. Damage is a "one-way" street. Like cancer and heart disease, RA needs early treatment before damage occurs. All progressive disease needs treatment as soon as possible.

Selective—Treat according to your needs and disease
In Chapter 2 we learned that RA cannot be considered a single disease: it has different types, or "temperaments." Each follows a different course and needs different treatment.

The three main types of RA are *mild, moderate,* and *severe.* To achieve the best long-term outcome, each type should be treated in a selective manner.

Unfortunately RA often gets treated in a uniform manner without allowances being made for the three distinct types. Each RA sufferer is unique. Size, sex, race, previous disease history, and other medical problems, make selective treatment more effective. Individual differences and resulting needs must be considered when developing a treatment plan.

Aggressive—Treat aggressively

Treatment with drugs singly, or in combination, at full therapeutic doses is essential for the best benefit. Full doses have the best chance of controlling RA. Combinations of the three drug types, NSAIDs, DMARDs, and steroids, often work better than a drug used singly, especially with the moderate and severe types of RA. Aggressive treatment prevents damage much more effectively than escalating treatment over time.

Persistent—Never quit

If a treatment program fails, the failure does not predict that another group of drugs will fail to control your RA. Different drugs act differently in different people. Each of us may have a slightly different response to inflammation, probably due to our unique genetic makeup, and this makes us more or less likely to react to various drug groups. Initial failure with one group tells us little, but the experience may make people feel discouraged, give up, or stop trying, exactly when an alterative plan should be started.

SELECTIVE TREATMENT PYRAMIDS
FOR THE DIFFERENT TEMPERAMENTS OF RA

A selective treatment program is used with each temperament! Within each selective treatment pyramid are alternatives in the NSAIDs or DMARDs. Open and frank conversation with your doctor helps establish your RA temperament. Then choices can be made within the selective treatment pyramid. The treatment target gives an overall perspective of how these drugs are used generally in all patients, but not how to use them specifically in particular cases. The treatment pyramids show how the three drug groups, NSAIDs, DMARDs, and steroids, and the health care professional team can be selectively used for your particular temperament of RA. Where you start on the treatment pyramid, depends on your RA temperament. Milds start with NSAIDs or mild DMARDs. Moderates always start with DMARDs or even combination DMARDs. Severes, in my view, should always start with combination DMARDs.

Mild Rheumatoid Arthritis

Mild RA is characterized by mild joint inflammation, some extra-articular features, and a low, or absent, rheumatoid factor. Most patients with mild disease will always have the mild form of the disease, and only rarely will they suffer any joint damage. In many patients, mild RA is sporadic, characterized by flare-ups and subsequent remissions. In mild disease, the main aim of therapy is to stop the inflammation with the milder, safer drugs, particularly the NSAIDs, and when required (i.e., during a flare-up), a DMARD. The selective treatment pyramid for mild RA is shown in Figure 9–1.

Most mild RA responds well to NSAIDs. The NSAID "STAR$" should be used at full therapeutic dose on a once or twice daily basis. In most patients with this type of RA, a significant improvement in the course of the disease should occur. Often drug therapy is continued for a few months to a few years. During this time, the disease will be held in check.

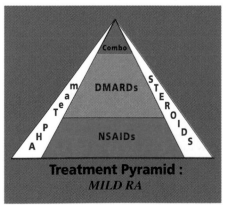

Treatment Pyramid :
MILD RA

Figure 9–1: The treatment pyramid for mild RA

If the RA persists, however, a first-level DMARD must be added to ensure that damage is prevented. Each rheumatologist has a personal favorite. Mine would be hydroxychloroquine (Plaquenil) added to the NSAID currently taken. Many physiotherapists and doctors recommend the use of a DMARD at the outset, an approach I encourage most patients to take. Alternatives could include sulfasalazine, methotrexate, or gold. For a significant flare-up, or to achieve early control, steroids may be helpful. The allied health professional team can be beneficial.

Moderate Rheumatoid Arthritis

Moderate rheumatoid arthritis makes up approximately 30% to 50% of all RA. In moderate RA, the arthritis is marked and often accompanied by extra-articular features, such as tendonitis or nodules. The rheumatoid factor is moderately to strongly positive in most, but not all, patients.

In the past, most patients with moderate disease eventually developed damage to the joints and tissue. During the past 20 years, DMARDs, which can bring about remission, have significantly changed the outcome for many patients. Moderate RA, can now usually be controlled, thus limiting the damage. We believe that moderate disease can be controlled by early and aggressive treatment, often combining NSAIDs, DMARDs, and steroids. The selective treatment pyramid for moderate disease is shown in Figure 9–2.

You will need a DMARD to get control of your arthritis. It

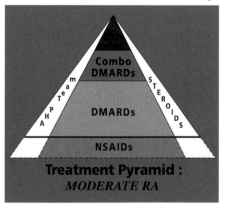

Figure 9–2: Treatment pyramid for moderate RA

could be methotrexate, gold, or hydroxychloroquine. If you have more aggressive disease, a combination of methotrexate and another DMARD, given with steroids and an NSAID, might be prescribed at diagnosis. You will also need the support and information of other health care professionals, including physiotherapists, occupational therapists, and social workers. Understanding the disease and how to handle it will improve your quality of life. You will require frequent follow-up visits that take into account the level of your disease. If one DMARD does not work, another should be tried immediately. Early, selective, aggressive treatment is required. Persistence until the disease can be controlled is essential.

Severe Rheumatoid Arthritis

Severe rheumatoid arthritis comprises 10% to 20% of patients. This is the type that has given RA its reputation as a "crippler." The severe type of disease is often, but not always, observed at its onset. Most patients with the severe type of RA progress relentlessly to significant damage of the joints and other tissues. The death rate in severe RA has been compared to that in coronary heart disease or cancer.

Over the past 20 years, the impact of treatment on severe RA has been minimal, and confusion about which drugs to use persists even now. Confusion leads to delay, lack of selectivity, and lack of aggression in using the currently available drugs. My approach to severe disease prescribes NSAIDs, steroids, and combination DMARDs, such as methotrexate with cyclosporine, hydroxychloroquine, or sulfasalazine, quickly and aggressively. I feel this gives the best chance for bringing the disease under control (Figure 9–3). Your family may also need help and emotional support. With severe disease, extensive support from allied health professionals is needed early. Hospitalization for rest, therapy, and intra-

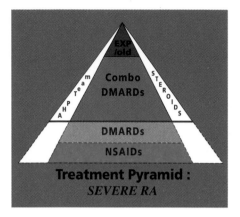

Figure 9–3: Treatment pyramid for severe RA

venous steroid treatment may be recommended.

The best approach to treating severe disease is as yet unclear, but we do know that delay or doing nothing leads to crippling. Patients with severe RA need to be seen every 2 weeks or monthly, until the disease is brought under control. If DMARDs in combination do not work, then other DMARDs or the new experimental drugs should be tried. The challenge in severe RA is to put out the inflammatory "fire."

SUMMARY

In this chapter, we have discussed the selective treatment pyramids for the three main temperaments of rheumatoid arthritis. We know that, within each pyramid, the treatment principles, **early**, **selective**, **aggressive**, and **persistent**, apply. Significant differences between the treatment approach to mild, moderate, and severe disease must be considered. Nonsteroidal anti-inflammatory drugs, DMARDs, and steroids should be harmonized appropriately. You with your doctor must make informed choices as to what would be the best treatment in your particular case. Lack of focus, delay in getting treatment, and slow or inappropriate treatment will seriously handicap the proper management of your disease, and your long-term prognosis (outcome) will be jeopardized.

COMMON MISTAKES

1. Offering the same treatment to everyone.

   Although popular belief is that everyone is the same, RA should not be treated in the same way. Selective treatment recognizes there are important differences among patients with RA.

2. Lack of persistence in trying different treatment regimens.

   Enthusiasm wanes with failure. Persistence, despite ongoing disease is essential to limiting the damage and disability of RA. Unfortunately the terms used to characterize RA are confusing. Terms such as early, late, chronic, prolonged, active, intercurrent, or end-stage are only some of these. These terms do not suggest that treatment could help. Patients may consider their cases hopeless. The term "progressive," however, means that further treatment is necessary and persistence in treatment is beneficial.

A SECOND OPINION

Since the disease can be extremely aggressive, the treatment of rheumatoid arthritis needs to begin early and should be aggressive. The analogy to a fire in the joints is a good one. Remember that, when putting out a fire, you must do it quickly, before the house burns down, and if a watering can doesn't work, then you need a hose – the bigger the better.

This analogy reflects the current trend to treating RA. The time to act is early, since most of the damage to joints takes place in the first 2 years. Holding off effective drug therapy until deformity or disability appear makes no sense. The practice of slowly adding drugs while the fire roars, misses a golden opportunity to control the disease and prevent damage. It is my current practice to begin aggressive therapy as soon as a diagnosis of RA is made. This has been referred to as inverting the pyramid, whereby, rather than adding drugs over time, if the patient does not respond, several drugs are started at once, and the most dangerous ones withdrawn once inflammation is controlled. For example, I begin therapy with an NSAID, plus hydroxychloroquine, plus methotrexate, and often prednisone. I then stop the prednisone as soon as inflammation is controlled, and over time, I stop the methotrexate. If things work perfectly, then the patient may require only the hydroxychloroquine to control the disease. Early experience with this approach has demonstrated that it works and that side effects have not been the problem we anticipated.

I find little to disagree with in the Bensens' approach to managing the patient with RA, and I can't stress enough the importance of the patient's role in this disorder. Do not accept arthritis as a diagnosis, since there are over a hundred different types of arthritis, with various outcomes and different therapies. Once the diagnosis *is* made, do not accept that nothing much can be done or that it is too soon to begin a drug that can effectively control inflammation. There are a few more points I would like to make:

1. Prednisone is a two-edged sword in that, as well as being very effective in controlling inflammation, it can cause significant side effects over time. If needed it should be used for as brief a time as possible, in as low a dose as possible, and with protection against osteoporosis.

2. Dr. Bensen's NSAID STAR$ are excellent drugs, but the best drug is the one that works for you without causing problems. Many patients do very well with the "other" NSAIDs.

3. Protection against ulcers is vital. Patients usually assume that if they have no symptoms they are fine, but this is not true. The first sign of a problem may be bleeding. Therefore it is important that the patients at greatest risk, as described by Dr. Bensen, receive prophylaxis.

4. Patients don't like taking drugs, and when necessary, try to take as small a dose as possible. In RA, control of inflammation is the top priority. In smaller doses the NSAIDS can provide pain relief, but little anti-inflammatory effect. The patient feels better, but the fire smolders. It is important to take the full dose as prescribed, and if side effects occur, to try another drug.

5. RA is a lifelong disease in the vast majority of patients. The most important member of the treatment team is you the patient. This book provides you with the basis to understand the disease and its treatment and thus to assure that you receive the best care currently available.

Gunner Kraag, M.D., F.R.C.P.
Chief, Division of Rheumatology
Ottawa Civic Hospital
Professor of Medicine
University of Ottawa

CHAPTER TEN

WHERE DO WE GO FROM HERE?

We have discussed rheumatoid arthritis in chapters 1 through 9; what it is, why it is important, how to diagnose it, and how to treat it. The gap between what could be accomplished and what is usually achieved with treatment still remains very wide! This "treatment (therapeutic) shortfall" is why RA remains the most common, treatable disability in the western world and one of the most misunderstood of diseases.

Rheumatoid arthritis can be controlled in most patients, especially if treated early. However, all patients with RA, early or late, with progressive disease should be treated selectively, aggressively and persistently. TREATMENT MAKES A REAL DIFFERENCE!

The main problem with RA treatment is delay—for diagnosis and for treatment. We hope this book will arm you with the facts you need to avoid delay and get the right treatment now. Delay is akin to "malpractice," yet is tolerated by most patients and is a feature of our health care system. You need to be "treated at the front of the line" just like you would be if you had cancer or heart disease.

To be treated effectively you need to see a physician who understands RA—how to recognize and diagnose it, and how to characterize and treat it. We have NSAIDs, DMARDs, and steroids that make a real difference. Although many people fear these drugs, they should fear the disease more. Only drugs make an important difference in preventing damage and disability. Getting little or no therapy is the worst option.

The future looks bright. The research of the past couple of decades has brought about a real change in our understanding and treatment. The research of today, supported by your tax dollars and contributions, will make a real difference over the next decade. We are currently testing new drugs, which are better and safer than those currently available. Rheumatologists are enthusiastic about the new opportunities these advances offer!

These days, many people are suspicious of doctors. They hear daily reports of the weaknesses or misconduct of doctors. Some are true, but many are perpetrated by those who do not understand health care or may benefit personally from the downgrading of physicians. A whole industry in rheumatoid arthritis perpetuates the idea that the disease is incurable and that doctors will treat you only for their own gain. As a result, alternatives are offered, which are expensive for you, yet have no proven benefit.

I can only say that, after 20 years of working with rheumatologists in Canada and other countries, I remain convinced of their sincere commitment to make a difference in the treatment of RA.

We hope this book will be a road map to help you navigate through the health care system. We believe that the models of management and treatment we present here can make a real difference if you have rheumatoid arthritis. Remember, you are the "captain of the team" and can make the choices which will allow the best outcome for you.

NEVER, NEVER, GIVE IN.

INDEX

Prednisone, 65, 67-68, 72, 84
Pregnancy, 6
Progressive nature of rheumatoid arthritis, 23, 25, 32, 37, 83
Prostaglandin production, 44, 46, 48
Pseudogout, 2, 30
Psoriasis, 29-30
Pyramid approach to rheumatoid arthritis. See Treatment pyramids

Quality of life, 19-20, 81

Redness, 29
Referrals, 26-27, 33, 36
Relafen™, 49
Remission, spontaneous, 37
Renal damage. See Kidneys
Research on rheumatoid arthritis, 61-62, 86-87
Rest, 65, 73
Rheumatoid arthritis:
  causes, 5-6
  change in type over time, 11
  classification, 9-14, 79-82
  common mistakes in diagnosis, 25, 35
  common mistakes in treatment, 23, 25, 35, 83-84
  "cure" for, 34, 38, 43-44
  diagnosis, 23, 25, 28-32
  duration, 10
  extra-articular features (EAFs), 10, 12, 14-16, 20, 28, 79
  incidence, 3-8, 36
  mild, 79-80
  moderate, 80-81
  onset of, 3, 7, 36
  progressive nature of, 23, 25, 32, 37, 83
  recurrence, 12
  remission, 37
  severe, 81-82

symptoms, 4-5, 12-20
"temperaments," 9, 11, 32, 77-78
tests for, 10-14, 30-31
Rheumatoid factor, in blood, 10, 12-14, 30-31, 80
Rheumatologists, 33, 36-37, 86-87

Sedimentation rate or "Sed rate." See Erythrocyte sedimentation rate
Self-help groups, 75-76
Septra™, 57
Sexual activity, 22, 74
Shortness of breath, 20
Side effects. See Adverse reactions to drugs
Skin rashes, 29, 47, 59, 60, 69
Smoking, 47
Social workers, 74, 81
Specialists. See Rheumatologists
Spinal cord, 18
Splints, 69, 73
Steroids, 39-41, 47, 64-65, 67-72, 78-82, 84, 86
Stiffness, 12-14, 20
Stomach pain, 60. See also Gastrointestinal problems
Stomach ulcers, 46-47, 50
Stress, 6, 74, 76
Stretch marks, 69
Stroke, 72
Sulfasalazine, 53, 55, 58, 60, 63, 80-81
Sulindac™, 48, 51
Support groups, 73-76
Suppositories, 43
Surgam™, 49
Swimming. See Pool therapy
Synovial fluid assessment, 31
Synovial joints, 1, 4
Synovial membrane, 2, 5, 7, 15

Synovitis, 15

Tear ducts, 19
"Temperaments" of rheumatoid arthritis, 9, 11, 32, 77-78
Tenderness of joints, 29
Tendonitis, 12-14, 20, 28, 30, 80
Tendons, 15-16
Tenosynovitis, 15
Tenoxicam™, 51
Tetracycline, 61
Therapy. See Drug therapy, Physiotherapy, Pool therapy, Occupational therapy
Thrombocytopenia, 59
Tiredness. See Fatigue
Treatment pyramids:
  mild, 79
  moderate, 80
  severe, 81-82
  inverted, 84
"Treatment target," 40
Treatment shortfall, 86
Triamcinolone, 67-68
Tuberculosis, 58

Ulcers, stomach, 46-47, 50, 84
Ultradol, 49
Ultrasound, 17
Urine tests, 59

Vasculitis, 19
Viral arthritis, 30
Vision disturbances, 54. See also Eyes
Vitamin D, 70, 72
Vitamins, 75
Voltaren™, 48, 49

Weakness, 13
Weight loss, 19, 29, 75
Weight gain, and steroids, 69, 70, 71
Women, risk of rheumatoid arthritis for, 36